THE
SILENT
ROOTS

K. M. GEORGE

THE SILENT ROOTS

ORTHODOX PERSPECTIVES ON CHRISTIAN SPIRITUALITY

Risk
BOOK SERIES

WCC Publications, Geneva

Cover design: Edwin Hassink

ISBN 2-8254-1147-7

© 1994 WCC Publications, World Council of Churches,
150 route de Ferney, 1211 Geneva 2, Switzerland

No. 63 in the Risk Book Series

Printed in Switzerland

To
ecumenical pilgrims —
my colleagues and students
at the
Bossey Ecumenical Institute

Table of Contents

Introduction

> I asked the tree,
> Speak to me of God,
> And it blossomed.
> — *Rabindranath Tagore*

The language of theology is infinitely richer than our well-constructed human speech and staggeringly more subtle than our linear logical reflection. If theology, as affirmed by the early tradition of the church, is primarily the spontaneous and thankful praise of God, the source of all life, then not only human beings but nature too theologizes. The Judaeo-Christian tradition acknowledged this truth by making the Psalms, with their cosmic praise of God, an essential part of liturgical prayer and theological meditation. Christian worship incorporated the whole creation in its doxology, the praise of the Triune God.

In our legitimate human quest for clear understanding, we run the risk of losing sight of the countless modes and possibilities of expressing theology, that is, of expressing our fundamental experiential relationship with God. In the name of theology the mystery of life is sometimes reduced to intellectually manageable categories. At this extreme point, theology may become some sort of "God-management". However, since God is easily eclipsed in contemporary secularized culture, theology can become at worst a management of nothingness and at best a collection of moral statements.

Any spirituality bonded to such notions of theology also becomes empty discourse. No stream of Christian theological tradition is immune to this danger in some form or other.

Theology understood as the worshipful experience of the Triune God and compassionate love for humanity and the whole creation has deep roots in the life of the church. It is Christian spirituality at its best. Here artificial academic distinctions between theology and spirituality do not apply.

With the onset of the environmental crisis, we have suddenly become conscious of "biodiversity". The great variety of life in our ecosphere, expressed by more than ten million known species of plants, animals and other organisms, is now consciously acknowledged by human beings to be pivotal for the health of the planet earth. However, this has always been part of the mystery of life whether we scientifically recognize it or not.

One could perhaps speak of a corresponding diversity in the interior realm of life as expressed by the innumerable roots, fruits and gifts of the Holy Spirit of God in creation. Perhaps the present spiritual crisis can make us aware of this inner spiritual diversity, as in the case of the external biodiversity. Yet, irrespective of our intellectual awareness of it, the Spirit has been distributing gifts from the beginning of creation.

It is not ultimately enough that we recognize and conserve the diversity of the biological life of millions of species as a "life-support service". We need to affirm with a profound faith conviction that this life has an orientation and that these different forms of the same life live together in mutually interconnected relationship and thus continually create our cosmic house into a living whole. The life of this organic house-body goes beyond the biological life of every species. This may not be an obvious truth for the scientist who recognizes biodiversity; but without the deep awareness of this dimension of the orientation of life, ecosystems will continue to suffer from human greed.

The presence of the church, the worshipping community that thankfully acknowledges God's life as trinitarian communion and continually calls upon the Holy Spirit to indwell and transform creation, has to symbolize this orientation for the biological as well as the spiritual life of the world. The Eastern Christian tradition still faithfully maintains the ancient practice of "orienting" the church building to the east, and the whole community together with the celebrants turns to the east for public worship. Orientation or symbolic turning to the source of light, to the sun of justice, to the original human experience of communion with God and nature, to the joyful light of the dawn of resurrection, is a dynamic gesture that sets the community in motion in a movement that constantly stretches forward.

The dichotomy between "institution" and "movement" with regard to the nature of the church may be transcended at the level of this oriented motion. Here not only the church but the whole creation is perceived to be in movement. There is nothing static or stable in this world on which the "rocky" foundation of the church can be laid. There is nothing so confident of permanence here against which the church can exclusively define itself as a movement either. The movement within the whole creation "for liberation from bondage to nothingness and for the glorious freedom of the children of God" (Rom. (8:21) has to be acknowledged as the proper setting for the church. This movement is for orientation, for "the turning around" (*metanoia*) to the source of light in a constant struggle against the power of darkness and all its expressions in our world.

The traditional language of pilgrimage — of the state of being an uprooted foreigner — hints at this fundamental perception of the whole creation in movement. The image of God in humanity assumes a significant role in guiding this movement because, as the tradition of the church affirms, human freedom and creativity are the principal expressions of the image. This image, the stamp of God's love and freedom in us, fully manifested in Christ, is our stronghold in the struggle against the powers of evil and the degradation of life. Like Abraham, the pilgrim-traveller offering hospitality to the strangers, the pilgrim church's hospitality to the creation-in-pilgrimage can transform this world into a place of theophany. The world's search for orientation in the desert of nothingness will find fresh meaning in this self-giving hospitality.

The oriented movement of humanity and the whole creation has to become an offering of love and thanksgiving to God. A thank-offering (*eucharistia*) in its deepest and best sense sums up Christian spirituality. It gathers up all the fruits of human nature and culture for offering with a profound awareness of the silent roots that sustain them.

Some of these reflections are taken up in this book. It is a modest attempt to recall to memory and re-order some significant yet currently marginalized dimensions of theology. It tries to see their implications for some interrelated ecumenical issues like human language, the image of God in humanity, the environmental crisis, global community, Christian spirituality, dialogue and so on. This is done with a grateful sense of the unbroken and dynamic Tradition of the church, and so these reflections claim no particular originality. I only wish to acknowledge my deep thankfulness to the innumerable men, women and children who interpret that Tradition in silence and in compassionate love.

Geneva, August 1994   *K.M. George*

1. The Naming of God

The inherent paradox of any theology, whether classical or contemporary, is that while God (*theos*), the chief subject of theology, is infinitely elusive and escapes all human language, there is always a torrent of words (*logos*) about God. Theologians have justified their use of words by appealing to such grounds as "God's self-disclosure in Christ the Word of God" and "the responsibility of the human mind gifted with the power of reason and speech". Yet we continue to suffer from the paradox of having to speak about the unspeakable. If theology is understood literally as a discourse on God ("God-talk"), with all its discursive ramifications, and if language becomes the medium par excellence of that discourse, then it is bound to produce much verbiage.

There have, however, been alternate visions of the vocation of theology, both in the past and the present. Contemporary theologians continue to raise the elementary question of whether there can be any systematic and rational clarification of God at all.[1] The word theology is sometimes rendered in modern English as "God-talk". But how meaningfully can we talk about God? What is the epistemological ground of what we call the discipline of theology? Is theology as God-talk possible at all? What is the relationship between God's revelation in Christ and our knowledge of God? It should be a sign of any healthy theologizing that the notion of theology is continually referred back to the primary question of its very legitimacy.

The question of God-language was central to the reflection of so-called classical theologians like the Cappadocian Fathers in the fourth century. They first encountered the problem of language about God in their effort to articulate the church's teaching on the trinitarian nature of God. In the contemporary context of a new anthropological awareness inspired by the feminist movement, the issue of "theo-linguistics" has assumed new dimensions of significance previously unknown to the Christian tradition. The two are closely interrelated and constitute a fundamental problem of theology.

The classical problematic drew attention to the infinite transcendence of God's being, which constantly undermines any cognitive optimism of the human mind or speech in relation to God. The preoccupation was with the process of eliminating all positive statements that might pretend to circumscribe or define the deity in any conceptual or anthropomorphic categories. While this concern with God's nature continues, the contemporary focus seems to be on what our God-language tells us about human nature and what it implies for such issues as gender, sexuality, inclusivity, justice and the shaping of a new spirituality.

The self-emptying intellect

Theology as faith seeking understanding (*fides quaerens intellectum*) has been of decisive significance for the Western Christian tradition. Generations of theologians have produced immense volumes in the sincere conviction that the chief task of theologians of the church is to provide an *intellectus fidei*, an understanding of faith, by making full use of the most distinctive human faculty, the power of reason.

In the Eastern Christian tradition, we do not generally encounter any similar principle encouraging theologians to elaborate on their discourse on faith. It is true that systematic Christian reflection in the East had largely stagnated by the time scholastic systematization of theology in the medieval West started its triumphal procession. The rift between the Latin West and the Greek East kept both traditions from any fruitful theological interaction until the rise of modern ecumenism.

Raimundo Panikkar, the Indian-Spanish Roman Catholic theologian, observes that the Indo-European civilizations in general have given an almost exclusive importance to the logos as *verbum mentis* or intelligibility, so that the most common feature of Christian theology has been that of understanding the logos as rational intelligibility. Orthodox theology and spirituality have also seen the icon in the logos and stress again and again the holistic nature of the logos and the mystical dimension of theology.[2]

Panikkar also offers an insightful comparison of the Western and Indian intuitions of being. He suggests that the deepest intuition of the Western tradition since Parmenides has to do with the intrinsic and co-extensive relation between thinking and being.

Thinking tells us what being is, and thus unfolds or discovers the truth [*aletheia*] of things; thinking gives us the ultimate trust [truth] that we walk on firm ground when we are rational [science] and reasonable [ethics]. The organ of this thinking is logos. Theology is consequently that ultimate human wisdom which is acquired when the human being thinks about his ultimate situation, taking into account all the data given to him, especially those given by a special disclosure of the divine Mystery itself.[3]

In the Indian perspective, according to Panikkar, the ultimate concern is not to know or think about being, but to let it be. Liberation is identified with this "letting being be", and there is no dichotomy between subject and object or knower and known. It is self-refulgent [*svayamprakasa*] pure awareness. As that participation in the unself-conscious awareness of the Theos, theology is not primarily a science but a mode of being. Here the Eastern Christian tradition comes close to the Indian spiritual-theological insight.

The Buddhist scholar and philosopher Masao Abe refers to the famous Christ-hymn in Philippians 2:5-8 as "one of the most impressive and touching passages in the Bible":[4]

Let the same mind be in you that was in Christ Jesus,
who, though he was in the form of God,
did not regard equality with God
as something to be exploited,
but emptied himself,
taking the form of a slave,
being born in human likeness.
And being found in human form,
he humbled himself
and became obedient to the point of death —
even death on a cross.

Abe argues that this self-emptying or kenosis should not be understood in a temporal or sequential order to mean that Christ was originally the son of God, then emptied himself and became identical with human beings. To him this would imply a conceptual and objectified understanding. Instead, he advocates an experiential and religious approach, understanding kenosis "to mean that Christ as the son of God is essentially and fundamentally self-emptying or self-negating — because of this fundamental nature, the son of God is Christ — is Messiah".[5]

Our usual Christian reading of the Philippians text tends to confine the kenotic character of God to the incarnate reality of Christ and inevitably to introduce a temporal sequence into our understanding of God's self-giving. It is true that the self-emptying nature of God is manifested in a unique way in the economy of incarnation. But the insistence of the Buddhist reader on the essential and fundamental self-negating of the son of God opens our eyes to a deeper dimension of Pauline kenotic theology seldom emphasized by Christian theologians. In spite of the recurrent liturgical reminder of "the Lamb slain before the foundation of the world" (Rev. 13:8) and the mystery of kenosis at the very heart of trinitarian love and divine economy, Christian theologians largely ignore the centrality of kenosis in our understanding of God and more particularly in our language about God.

Self-negation of discourse is thus foundational to true theology. Having denied itself, theology cannot fall back upon its own logos or logic to become a discursive exercise. It must transcend itself. Every self-negation becomes a fresh act of self-transcending. "Concepts make idols of God," said the fourth-century Christian theologian and philosopher Gregory of Nyssa. Any affirmative concept of God can become an idol that creates an iron curtain between God and us.

Eastern Christian tradition generally associates the kenotic self-negation of theology with the apophatic or negative way. An apophatic approach to God necessarily transcends the conceptual and the verbal. It points to the antinomies and paradoxes that arise when conceptual language attempts to conceive of and articulate the essential mystery of God's being. Although expressions like "mystical theology" and "the apophatic way" are rightly associated with the writings of Dionysius the Areopagite, who was probably a fifth-century Syrian monk whose writings became enormously popular both in East and West, it is in the concerted work of the three fourth-century Cappadocian theologians — Basil of Caesarea, Gregory of Nazianzus and Gregory of Nyssa — that one finds an original and balanced view of the apophatic approach to theology.

Moses' vision of darkness

A significant image in Cappadocian thinking is that of the biblical account of Moses going up Mount Sinai in order to meet Yahweh (Ex. 33:17-23). These theologians see a clear evolution in the spiritual growth of Moses on the basis of his experience of

God. At the time when Moses was going around as a shepherd, having already been through the sophisticated wisdom of the Egyptians in Pharaoh's court, he received the first theophany in a burning bush (Ex. 3:1-4:17). God appeared to him as powerful light — the light of a blazing fire that inflamed the green bush without burning it. It was visible light, perceptible to the senses, though the deity retained its essential mystery in the puzzling words "I am who I am" (3:13-15). Moses was still at the foot of the spiritual ladder.

Then he rose, over the years, to become the great charismatic leader and supreme spiritual figure of Israel. It was at this stage of deep spiritual experience and wisdom that he was asked to go up the holy mountain to receive the ten commandments. On Mount Sinai Moses went into "thick darkness". He experienced God not in the rational, sensible visibility of light as in his immature years, but in the total negation of any perception — physical or intellectual.

This interpretation is firmly rooted in the philosophical and spiritual tradition of the Alexandrian school of theology in the East. The apophaticism inherent in this theological-hermeneutical heritage is radicalized in the writings of Dionysius the Areopagite, with the help of strong Neo-platonic elements:

> Leave the senses and the workings of the intellect, and all that the senses and the intellect can perceive, and all that is not and that is; and through unknowing reach out, so far as this is possible, towards oneness with him who is beyond all being and knowledge. In this way, through uncompromising, absolute and pure detachment from yourself and from all things, transcending all things and released from all, you will be led upwards towards that radiance of the divine darkness which is beyond all being. Entering the darkness that surpasses understanding, we shall find ourselves brought, not just to brevity of speech, but to perfect silence and unknowing. [6]

Gregory of Nazianzus (330-390), known as "the theologian" in the tradition of the church, is thoroughly fascinated, like his friend Gregory of Nyssa, by the dark vision of Moses. He refers to the two Exodus passages narrating the vision of Moses to illustrate his point about the total incomprehensibility of God. [7] The first is Exodus 20:21: "Then the people stood at a distance, while Moses drew near to the thick darkness where God was."

Gregory interprets this darkness that surrounds God, "who made darkness his covering around him" (Ps. 18:11), as the inherent incapacity of created nature to penetrate the essential mystery of God. He uses the image of a veil to describe this darkness, which separates created nature from the uncreated. It should be pointed out that this veil of incomprehensibility is not considered a moral deficiency in humanity but as constitutive of all created reality, including spiritual and angelic beings. Sometimes the veil is matter in general, sometimes it is the material human body and sometimes it is the usual intellectual categories of human knowing. Apparently the screen or veil of darkness hinders the vision of God's nature and is negative as far as human intellect is concerned. But it has a salutary function which is decisive for Gregory's understanding of theology. This leads to his reference to Exodus 33:22, where the incident of Moses' vision in the cleft of the rock is narrated.

Moses earnestly desires to see God face to face though he is told that this would be absolutely impossible. He persists and so he is granted a "vision". In the biblical account he is made to stand and wait inside the cleft of a rock. A mighty hand covers the opening of the cleft and God's glory passes by. Moses could see only "the back parts of God" (*ta hopisthia*), the vestiges of glory that were left trailing behind. Apparently the desire of Moses is not fulfilled. He is denied direct and first-hand vision. He was however protected by the rock because, as God said to him, "you cannot see my face; for no one shall see me and live" (v.20). The rock has a two-fold purpose here: to hide Moses's complete vision and thus to save him from a fatal exposure to a total vision of the deity.

Gregory interprets this rock which hides and thus saves Moses as the incarnate Christ. Translating this to his own mystical experience, he says: "And then when I looked up, I hardly saw the back parts of God, although I was sheltered by the rock, the word that was made flesh for us."[8] This idea is central to Gregory's understanding of the vocation of the bodily or incarnate person of Christ who shares our materiality. The incarnate Christ acts as a dark veil that hides from human beings any intellectual knowledge of the essential nature of God. But this hiding and negation are supremely salutary because they protect the aspirant from a debilitating vision and show the seeker after truth an entirely new way of salvation. Thus in contrast to an understanding of the flesh of Christ as "the window through which the Lord showed himself",[9] Gregory would rather consider the flesh of Christ in a uniquely soteriological perspective as a saving curtain which covers the window of any rational comprehension.

The Cappadocians would affirm that in its aspect of hiding, the incarnate physical body of Christ really participates in our material and created condition. A characteristic mark of this condition is that the knowledge of God's true nature is opaque to it. This explains the weakness of the incarnate Christ, his humble form as a servant, his ignorance and many other human limitations which the Arian teachers considered a clear sign of his subjection and ontological subordination to God the Father.[10] As defenders of the Nicene faith, the Cappadocian Fathers, standing in a solid tradition of the church, affirmed that these "weaknesses" of the incarnate Son of God were real, but they were signs of the total identification of God in Christ with the creation in the most self-emptying way and were therefore essential features of the mystery of incarnation. They were salutary and were to be understood as God's means of saving us, not as grounds for dialectical arguments to undermine the church's teaching about the Holy Trinity.

In a very general way one may identify within the history of Christian spirituality and theological reflection two parallel trends which appear to be mutually exclusive, but in fact are not. On the one hand is the strong continuing current of an apophatic attitude to the question about God, which aspires to overcome the verbal or conceptual logos — though without minimizing the intellectual dimension, as we see in the Cappadocians — in order to contemplate the ineffable mystery of God in total silence. This attitude is largely represented in the ascetic-monastic tradition and is very often too sweepingly qualified by Western theologians as the "mystical approach". On the other hand is a powerful cognitive tradition of interpreting in intelligible words what is known about God in Christ on the authority of biblical testimony and the tradition of the Christian community. The human gift of discursive reasoning, various forms of ecclesiastical authority, the direct spiritual experience of individuals and other forms of knowledge are all used in this act of interpretation. This is what is traditionally called theology in the usual sense of the word. This kind of cognitive, descriptive and rational approach to theology became normative in the West in the wake of the brilliant intellectual heritage of Augustine, the medieval scholastic enterprise of rational and systematic discourse on God and the Reformation emphasis on the preached word of God.

In the former approach, logos is transcended in the pursuit of the experience of God, an experience that is shrouded in almost total silence. In the latter, logos is consciously resorted to as the medium par excellence to express the content of revelation in Christ and the experience of God. It is inaccurate to qualify the one as exclusively Eastern and the other as exclusively Western, for both tendencies appear in both East and West. But the difference in the degree of inclination to one or the other is considerable. The Eastern Christian tradition is extremely hesitant to make academic distinctions within theology ("dogmatic" theology, "mystical" theology, "biblical" theology and so on) despite the universal influence of the contemporary Western academic tradition. It would simply affirm that the fundamental apophatic approach to the mystery of God undergirds all articulations in theology. The "negative way" is not formally distinguished from a "positive way", but negation is considered to be constitutive of all positive affirmations on God. A good number of the theologians whose work contributed substantially to what we today call Eastern patristic theology were leading intellectuals of their time, trained in secular disciplines. They did not hesitate to use their secular learning in the service of the gospel of Christ or, as Gregory of Nazianzus put it, "to turn the bastard letters to the service of those that are true". [11]

On the basis of this patristic vision, we may distinguish three dimensions of "God-language", all equally important and integral to each other, which belong to the core of Eastern Christian tradition and which are relevant to such contemporary concerns as gender, inclusive language and ecumenical spirituality: the silence of theology, the speech of "economy" and the celebration of beauty.

1. The silence of theology

"Theologia", a non-biblical word of Greek literary-philosophical origin, acquired a new meaning in the writings of fourth-century Christian teachers like Athanasius of Alexandria and Gregory of Nazianzus. Primarily it came to be used as a synonym for the triune God, Father, Son and Holy Spirit.[12] Only secondarily and derivatively did it refer to discourse about God. Especially in Gregory of Nazianzus, the dialectical relationship between these two levels of "theology" became fundamental in understanding the language of theology.

In the primary sense of the term, as applied to the mystery of the triune God, God cannot be the object of any so-called theological discovery. In the radical transcendence and infinity of God's being, God can only be worshipped and not conceptually conceived in the mind or verbally described. Human beings stand in total silence in the overwhelming presence of the mystery. Any conceptual language about God does not just fall short of truth; it is absolutely impossible.

Here *theologia* stands for the inscrutable nature of God's essential being, ontologically hidden from all created beings, including angelic and spiritual beings. The patristic tradition maintains that this thick veil over human knowledge is not of an historical or moral order, to be removed at some later point, but constitutes the fundamental character of all created reality. This is no judgment on the cognitive gifts or intellectual attainments of the human mind, but rather signifies the absolutely incomprehensible nature of God's being, "the ocean without shores". It inspires an ultimate silence of being in the true seekers after truth.

Silence is usually understood as the absence of all external auditory stimulus, the hearing of no sound. Sound and silence are opposed to each other in a physical sense. However, this is not the sense in which we speak about silence in relation to theology. When Ignatius of Antioch calls Christ "the word that came out of the silence" of the Father, far from opposing word to silence he is expressing the integral connection between them. In a particularly religious sense, the hearing of the word is not opposed to silence. It is perceived to originate in a profound and mysterious silence. In the Indian religious-philosophical tradition, *ohm*, the primal sound at the source of all reality, arises from the depth of perennial silence. It is equated to the ultimate principle of creativity. The word resounds from silence and returns to silence. In the Zen Buddhist tradition, natural sounds like that of the waterfall are not considered to be opposed to silence but on the contrary contribute to the deep silence of the spiritual aspirant in meditation. Here sound is assimilated into the overall harmony of profound religious experience.

The word of God, as read or expounded by human agents, does not constitute an obstacle to silence, but contributes to the experience of silence. This is possible because of the conviction underlying all religious discourse that every word must return to its matrix of silence. It finds meaning and fulfilment only when it returns to its source of origin. In our ordinary language a "vain" or an "empty" word is one that cannot perform an action and is therefore simply lost. An efficient word is one that returns and reports to the speaker, the source, after having performed its mission. The centurion points this out to Jesus, comparing his own word of authority as centurion to that of Jesus as divine healer (Matt. 8:5-13). Jesus is understood by the writer of the fourth gospel as the word of God that returns to God after having accomplished the mission of salvation. Jesus himself saw his return to the Father as constituting an essential aspect of his mission in the world.

Speech and silence in ordinary theologizing are often determined by the spirit of the age. In our contemporary culture, dominated by the written and spoken word, silence is often misunderstood as the inability of the human mind to express itself. In an academic culture that dictates to teachers of theology "publish or perish" there is no way to relate silence to theology without being misunderstood as "mystical" if not weird. Some streams of the Reformation tradition, placing an almost unilateral emphasis on the preached word, have not always taken sufficient account of the power and wealth of silence. Preachers generally do not dwell on the silence of Jesus. They interpret only the "activist" side of his ministry — his words and deeds — and say little if anything about the many nights Jesus spent alone in silence and prayer in a solitary place away from the crowd and from his own close disciples. Some of our highly vociferous preachers apparently find no edifying material in the gospel narratives about the forty days of fasting and prayer in solitary silence which Jesus observed before his public ministry or his closing of the lips on some of the crucial occasions in his public life.

In the West the Christian attitude, shaped in the context of Enlightenment rationality, became suspicious of silence. Silence is accused of evading Christian responsibility. Silence is sinful. Silence is oppressive. The stigma attached to silence has been carried over to our present age, in which any Christian concern for human rights is supposed to be expressed primarily in statements. Persons and communities that maintain silence are automatically looked down upon as collaborators in human oppression. Nobody seems to care for the self-imposed kenotic silence of many martyrs and the silence of all those women and men who shed tears of compassion and prayed in silence for the transformation of tragic human situations. Of course, these are not always mutually exclusive. But an excessive concern with stating the truth in words is perhaps to be seen as corresponding to a scholastic and intellectualist notion of theology that has prevailed over all other expressions of the experience of God. This obsession, strengthened by the modern media culture, has definitely contributed to the devaluation of silence.

The word-centred rationality of the dominant culture has even eliminated many possibilities for silence. Naturally, theology, caught within the framework of this culture, is obliged to become rational discourse. This violates the harmony of experience authenticated in the tradition of religious experience in which the word spoken or written or the sound of natural phenomena does not disrupt the harmony of the whole.

What we learn and teach as theology today is therefore preeminently a cultural product, a systematic and rational reflection on God within the framework of the assumptions of the dominant culture which dictate the epistemological parameters and methodological-linguistic tools of our theology. Not that this tendency is anything new. Already in the patristic age, judging by some of the violent doctrinal debates that split the body of the one church asunder in the fifth century, one might say that the apophatic sense of the relativity and reserve of theological language with regard to the mystery of God's incarnation seems to have been replaced on both sides by an excessive confidence in the correctness of the terminology they were using to set forth the mystery of the union of the divine and the human in the person of Christ.

Apophatic silence is profoundly kenotic. Far from being empty, it is full of spiritual riches. Foremost of these riches is compassion. The withdrawal of the external word occurs simultaneously with the radiation of a spiritual energy, a compassionate, consoling presence demonstrated in the lives of certain saintly persons in recent history like Ramana Maharshi in India or Seraphim of Sarov in Russia.

Apophatic silence is then the method of theology at this level. This silence spreads its veil not simply on our language, but on our mind and reason, on our very being. The heart of ascetic-monastic spirituality is soaked in this silence. The spirituality of the desert has many stories about silence. *The Sayings of the Desert Fathers* relates the visit of Theophilus, Archbishop of Alexandria, to the desert of Scetis. The brothers assembled to receive him and asked Abba Pambo, a well-known spiritual father, to say something to the archbishop so that he might be edified. The old man said to them: "If he is not edified by my silence, he will not be edified by my speech."[13]

Metropolitan Anthony Bloom, a contemporary Orthodox spiritual father, qualifies these ascetics in a felicitous phrase as "men and women wrapped in a depth of inner silence of which we have no idea and who taught by 'Being' and not by speech".[14]

It is significant that this exercise of silence as the proper way of true theology oriented to experience was never considered as the method exclusively of ascetics in the desert, but it became the ideal of theology in such "official" theologians of the church as the Cappadocians. They, unlike the anchorites in seclusion, were thoroughly involved in the heated theological debates with the Arian and Eunomian teachers in the fourth century, and so were bound to speak and write prolifically in defence of the faith of the church. The more they were dragged into speaking, the more they put the accent on the normative character of silence in theology.

Their grappling with the issue of silence and speech led them to the following: Every theological enterprise in the sense of a rational-verbal discourse on God is a highly relative one.

Gregory of Nazianzus gives a relative and deliberately minimal definition of a theologian:

> Our best theologian is he who has, not indeed discovered the whole, for our present chain does not allow of our seeing the whole, but conceived of God to a greater extent than another, and gathering in himself more of the likeness or adumbration of the truth, or whatever we may call it. [15]

2. Economy of speech

The second level of God-language can be called the language of economy (*oikonomia*). It is positive and affirmative and arises from the incarnate reality of the Christ-event. "The Word became flesh and lived among us, and we have seen his glory, the glory as of a father's only son, full of grace and truth" (John 1:14). In affirming this faith in the incarnate Word and in proclaiming and witnessing to his glory, we may use all the intellectual and spiritual gifts of humanity. At this level faith seeks understanding and seeks to interpret that understanding to the world. Here theology becomes a vocation and demands a commitment. No area of life is impervious to this act of theologizing and no tool of human reason and knowledge totally useless for its incessant search. Yet it is a language of economy — veiled, reserved and prudent — and its ultimate destiny is total silence.

The word *oikonomia* has always been used in the patristic tradition as a synonym of the incarnation of God in Christ. *Oikonomia* is literally "home rule", a way of governing one's own household from within. It implies a method that is different from the often legalistic, impersonal and imposing ways of public administration. Economy or home rule is based on a method of self-limitation and accommodation. In dealing with created humanity, God assumed the method of humble and sacrificial self-giving, "taking the form of a slave" (Eph. 2:7). This compassionate accommodation on the part of God to the condition of created reality was to bring the alienated creation to its original harmony. So *oikonomia* became the method of *theologia*, as the ineffable and incomprehensible being of God became incarnate in Jesus of Nazareth, limiting himself to the conditions of birth and death. We may identify some of the major implications of these underlying patristic theological perceptions:

a) The incarnate condition of Christ or divine economy calls us to a freedom of speech which is both a gift and a task. It is a gift in the primary sense of our being granted boldness of access and speech (*parrhesia*) in the presence of God through Jesus our high priest (Heb. 4:16). It is a task, which again is not limited to any particular cultural or linguistic expressions of faith or to any parochial areas of human existence. This is true of human language as well. Within the economy of incarnation, we are called to exercise our reflective and imaginative faculties and invent language that is appropriate for the deepest spiritual experiences of humanity. It is common knowledge that culturally dominant languages appropriate to themselves the right to speak "rightly" about God. Depending on political-economic conditions Greek or Latin, Sanskrit or Syriac, Persian or Arabic assumed this role in different periods of history and in different contexts. In India until very recently Sanskrit was qualified as the "language of gods" (*deva bhasha*), and the brahmanic priestly class alone had the right to learn and recite the scriptures in that language. The members of the lowest castes or outcastes were denied the right to learn Sanskrit, and there were cases of active persecution of any low-caste person studying that language. The history of Christian doctrine also shows the exclusive association between certain dominant languages and the norms of right belief, thus underestimating if not totally denying diversity and the freedom of speech of other people to express their experience of faith in Christ.

b) The tradition of the church holds fast to certain expressions about God, like "Father", as authoritative on the ground that Jesus Christ in the incarnate condition used it and taught us to use it (Luke 11:1-2). The Orthodox, Catholic and some Protestant traditions have so far seen no ground to change that, since it is on the authority of Christ himself, attested to in the gospels. Whether that expression has been abused by institutional structures to support oppression is a different question, which the language of economy cannot by any means ignore. The difficulty is that any name of God, however authoritative, can be misconstrued by human agents to justify institutional attitudes that run counter to the love and justice of God. This is a problem inherent in our conceptual thinking and linguistic mode of perception. "Patriarchy," writes Dorothee Sölle from a feminist perspective, "easily confuses its concept of God, and does not understand that even the statement 'God is the father of all human beings' is a symbolic statement — and not a real description. The moment I make that a non-symbolic, i.e., a reified, dogmatic statement, which rules out other statements like 'God is the mother of all men and women', my thought of God is too small. I have reduced God to my spiritual horizon and shut God up there."[16]

From the point of view of the language of economy dear to the patristic tradition, one need not necessarily disagree with this statement while at the same time pointing out that the title "mother" can also be instrumentalized by any dominant ideology to exclude other possibilities. Therefore the patristic tradition, while sticking to the authority of Jesus' calling God "Father", would immediately remind us that Jesus used the human analogy of father and son within the accommodative, self-limiting human condition of incarnation or economy. So it is an economic speech, which we have either to retain within the realm of economy or push off to the first level of theology, namely total silence. As Gregory of Nazianzus puts it, "The names Father and Son do not belong to us in an absolute sense. For we are both."[17]

The ambiguity in the possibility for a human male to be a father and a son at the same time stands between our concept of the fatherhood of God and the reality of God which transcends all analogies and concepts. When the doctrine of the church affirms that God the Father is eternally Father and God the Son is eternally Son, we cannot simply project onto this our own experiential notions of fatherhood and sonship. Nicene orthodoxy stated that the distinctive hypostatic quality of God the Father is *agennesia*, "unborn-ness" or ingenerateness, and that of the Son is *genesis*, generateness, and that of the Holy Spirit is *ekporeusis*, "proceeding". So in the trinitarian doctrine, Father is not Son and Son is not Father, while in our biological experience one person can be both father and son at the same time. The language of economy fully recognizes this simple truth of a radical break between our biologically determined notions of fatherhood and the fatherhood of God, and upholds the authority of Christ in his use of the name father.

The fourth-century struggle of the church with the Arians and Eunomians was precisely over this. The heretical teachers, according to the defenders of Nicene faith, did not respect the difference between *theologia* and *oikonomia* and applied biological analogies and conceptual frameworks to the trinitarian mystery. So they strayed from the true faith when they spoke about the inferiority of the Son to the Father in a chronological-biological order or expressed their optimism about "knowing" the truth of God's essential nature by the use of humanly conceived names and notions. The orthodox teachers insisted that our environment necessarily intervenes in whatever we say about abstract realities. It is impossible to arrive at a "pure" notion of truth free of any human environment, just as it is impossible for a person to step over his shadow, for the eyes to see objects without light and for fish to glide outside water. [18]

So the principle of economy opens up our theological language about God to the virtually limitless possibilities of relating with the created reality, while resisting all attempts to absolutize that language, as it is precisely the language of economy.

Biblical-patristic tradition recognizes the metaphorical and symbolic function of God-language inasmuch as that language is rooted in the self-emptying humility of God in Christ. The mystery of *kenosis* does not sustain any triumphalist and discriminatory language. Some of the best spiritual streams in both West and East have always used the criterion of compassion and humility, "a moist heart", to get beyond the so-called imperialist or patriarchal discourses in regard to God.

A compassionate heart can easily recognize the ocean of meaning that surges beneath the metaphors used for God, like father, mother, lover or friend, and it can invent many more. Sallie McFague points out that one of theology's primary tasks for our time is to "remythologize". This recognizes the metaphorical character of theology and rejects the demythologizing attempt to denude religious language of its concrete, poetic, imagistic and hence inevitably anthropomorphic character. Remythologizing theology is "identifying and elucidating primary metaphors and models from contemporary experience which will express Christian faith for our day in powerful illuminating ways".[19]

With a sane perception of the radically apophatic character of all theology and the committed God-language of incarnation (economy) we can fruitfully exercise our freedom and imagination in reflecting on new modes of human consciousness arising out of women's experience or growing awareness of ecological interdependence. This reflection will not thus easily fall into a new dogmatism of concepts, but stimulate more compassion and sense of solidarity. This is true not only for our times but was also perceived as such by the tradition of the church in relation to contemporary challenges. "The apophatic attitude," writes Vladimir Lossky, "gave to the Fathers of the church that freedom and liberality with which they employed philosophical terms without running the risk of being misunderstood or of falling into a theology of concepts."[20]

c) The core of the language of economy is experience — experience of the incarnate Son of God. Ultimately this experience eclipses all language. Between theology and economy, between the apophatic reality of the triune God and the "raw fact" of the incarnation, the connecting link is not discourse, but the experience of divinization, or, as the Greek language calls it, *theosis*. The concern to speak about God (*theologein*) is totally eclipsed by an overriding concern for "becoming God" (*theon genesthai*). This involves not only the transformation of our inner qualities and attitudes, but a transfiguration of our physical reality as well. The scope of true theology is the liberation of all created reality from its bondage to decay and the obtaining of "the freedom of the glory of the children of God" (Rom. 8:21). Christ the Saviour "will transform our humble bodies that they may conform to his glorious body" (Phil. 3:21).

In the spiritual tradition of the Eastern church, especially in the ascetic-monastic movement, we see a growing insistence on the eclipse of language in favour of an experience that defies expression. In fact the Eastern Christian tradition shares this trait with the other major spiritual traditions of Asia like Buddhism and Hinduism, in which a person with higher spiritual experience tends to be a *muni*, the ascetic who observes *mauna* or silence. The celebrated silence of Buddha about God has never been interpreted as really atheistic in Asian philosophical-spiritual traditions.

The emphasis on the experience of God at the expense of discourse about God in Eastern tradition has earned it the adjective "mystical". Although the expression "mystical theology" came originally from the East in the writings of Dionysius the Areopagite, it was popularized by Western theologians who were preoccupied with the rational articulation of theology. It is unfortunate that the essential experiential core of all theology is masked by a false distinction between "mystical theology" and other forms of academic theology.

The word "spirituality" has suffered a similar fate. In fact, Christian tradition has no equivalent for this rather recent word. Now it is being used in all sorts of contexts without any specific meaning, often as a kind of filler when one is groping for words in the course of a theological discourse. Current ecumenical documents distinguish "theology" from "spirituality".

Spirituality in its primary sense is simply faith-practice. Experience is its heart. At this primary level it excludes discourse. In this sense spirituality is not different from the perception of theology we have outlined above. The present danger is that spirituality at worst becomes a subject of verbal discourse, losing its meaning of experience, or at best gets divorced from theology as practice is divorced from theory. We will take up the issue of spirituality in more detail later in this book.

3. The celebration of beauty

The third essential dimension of authentic God-language is its relation to beauty and worship. This cultic-aesthetic dimension fuses together apophatic silence and economic speech in the liturgical acts of the faith community, characterized by joyful celebration and the luminous vision of beauty. Integrating the aesthetic into the liturgy and expressing the worship of God (*doxa*) through forms of beauty, the Eastern Christian tradition affirms the cultic-aesthetic experience as the essential locus of theology. It thus opens up vast possibilities of diverse and symbolic speech about God within the matrix of apophatic silence and engages all the senses in the creation and appropriation of beauty which illumines the dreary wastelands of our daily life in the light of its eschatological vision.

According to the Eastern tradition there is no theology without the experience of beauty. Dogmatic formulas are of no use if they are simply abstract propositions isolated from this doxological-aesthetic celebration, which continually creates beauty. So the liturgy as the heart of faith does not simply recite the creed, but celebrates the mystery of the death and resurrection of Christ, of our creation and redemption, of life in all its diversity and its transfiguration. The two basic doctrines of the church, namely the Trinity and the incarnation, are logically so self-contradictory that a rational discourse (*logos*) on them is a total impossibility. The church accepts them as subjects for teaching and learning (*dogma*) on condition that the ultimate word on them be silence. If we remove them from the realm of ordinary reason and logical speech, a whole new possibility opens up, that of worship, *doxa*, praising and celebrating the mystery of God.

Here we are far removed from any obsession with the word. Praising God can be with word or without word, in speech or in silence. The cultic and doxological element transcends logical categories of discourse, although it can still make use of them. There are, however, traditions in Christianity which seek to reduce the whole act of worship into neat and rigid frames of rationality. Obviously, the sense of mystery is missing in this type of worship; and the doctrines become a matter of instruction and logical reflection. The ultimate outcome is that the doctrines become at best dry statements without any opening for creative meditation, at worst meaningless. The elements of faith and mystery are not, however, fully subject to the analysis of reason. They are essentially rooted in a trans-logical silence.

The dialectic between speech and silence finds a creative resolution in the realm of the cultic and the poetic. A hymn attributed to Gregory of Nazianzus admirably exemplifies the paradox of speech and silence and how God is both "panonymous", having all names, and "anonymous", having no name. "The silent hymn" evokes simultaneously the apophatic silence and the hymnic utterance, both integral to the liturgical celebration:

O Thou, the beyond of all
(Is it not the only permissible praise
with which to address thee?),
How can the word sing praise to Thee,
Since no word can express Thee?
How can the mind perceive Thee,
Since no mind can perceive Thee?
Thou the only Unutterable,
For all that is uttered comes from Thee.
Thou the only Unknowable,
For all that is conceived comes from Thee.
All beings,
Those who are endowed with speech
And those who are deprived of word,
Proclaim Thee...
To Thee is raised a silent hymn
By all those who perceive Thy complexity.
For Thee alone exists everything,
To Thee all tend in a single block.
Thou art the end of all things.
Thou art One,
Thou art all, and Thou art none.
Thou art not one and Thou art not all.
O Thou who hast all the names,
How shall I name Thee?
Thou the only unnameable.
What celestial mind can penetrate Thy veil
which is far beyond the clouds even?[21]

The biblical image of the deity as luminous is central to the patristic theological and spiritual vision. How thoroughly the Johannine celebration of the image of light has penetrated the Eastern spiritual vision is clearly seen in Egyptian and Syro-Palestinian desert spirituality, the writings of seminal theologians like the Cappadocians, the hesychast tradition of Mount Athos, Russian spirituality, as well as in the liturgical texts and the practice of iconography. "God is light and in him there is no darkness at all" is the message John proclaims, which, he testifies, he and his fellow apostles heard from Jesus Christ himself (1 John 1:5). The incarnate image of that light was Christ himself. "The true light, which enlightens everyone, was coming into the world" (John 1:9). This glorious light has become the life of the world and so the whole creation now is animated by it. The highest spiritual aspiration in the Eastern view thus consists not only in walking in this light, which constitutes our ethical being, but in becoming light itself, participating fully in the divine glory.

The image of resplendent divine light is a visual symbol that relates the fleeting experience of beauty in our senses to the abiding beauty of heavenly Jerusalem through the incarnate image of Christ, "the image of the invisible God" and the "effulgence of God's glory". The destiny of creation is to become luminous and transparent to the source of all being. As one of the prayers of the Eastern church says: "O God, you started the work of creation with light in order that the whole creation may become light." The patristic vision of the mutually transparent choirs of angels that encircle and dance around the luminous throne of light and its confident faith in humanity's possibility to participate in this radiant choreography of beauty is not a metaphorical embellishment to theology, but it is theology at its best. This aesthetic vision is decisive for God-language, and it flows into an ensemble of colours, sounds, smell, taste, gestures and rites. The hope is that the thick, heavy matter that now weighs us down in various forms shall become incandescent by participation in the divine light. As Gregory of Nazianzus, the poet-theologian, says of the transfiguration of Christ, "it initiates us into the mystery of future". [22] The light of Tabor, the mount of transfiguration, is for Gregory and other teachers of the church the symbol par excellence of the beauty and goodness of created nature; and light signifies its final destiny as well. This aesthetic experience is unquestionably true to the essential meaning of incarnation, which signifies the participation of created nature in the experience of divinization, as formulated in the famous dictum of Athanasius that "God became a human being that human beings may become divine". The conviction that all matter, including inorganic matter, carries the potential of transfiguration underscores the sacramental vision and spiritual practice of the Eastern church.

"Respectable" academic theology often relegates the idea of transfiguration and the vision of beauty to the odd realm of "mystical theology". As Moltmann frankly admits, Western theology has paid little attention to transfiguration and placed the accent in an imbalanced way on God's power and dominion, rather than on divine splendour and beauty. This emphasis on the sovereignty of God placed Christian existence under legal and moral categories. The aesthetic categories of a new freedom disappeared in favour of the moral category of a new law and new obedience. [23]

Ultimately, refusal to accept as part of normative theological language about God images of beauty, of tenderness, of motherly compassion, of the many-voiced possibilities of poetic speech, of the illuminating power of symbols and metaphors is a denial of resurrection itself. If theology cannot break its own rigid conceptual frame, it cannot hint at any experience of beauty that transcends our logical — and very limited — perceptions of the historical order. We need what Paul Evdokimov has called *iconosophia*, the wisdom of the icons, [24] an openness and Spirit-inspired ability to image God in the infinity of God's own compassionate love, tenderness, goodness and freedom, and not in the image of our own distorted selves and institutional hierarchies. This wisdom has implications for what Metropolitan Paulos Gregorios calls *iconopoeia*, the creative possibility for us to make images of the future. [25]

The new search for an alternate God-language, for a different set of metaphors, by which to experience a God who is totally other than what some dominant theological and ecclesiastical traditions proclaim is understandable in the context of the alienation of those traditions from their roots in the Christ-experience and the authority structure built around that alienation. Patrick Sherry suggests that it would be interesting to speculate on how both "theological" and "aesthetic" have tended to become derogatory terms, especially considering that their parents, religion and art, are both supposed to be concerned with what is profound and moving in human life. [26] The simple response to this question is that both theological and aesthetic thinking have ceased to evoke any experience of God or of beauty because of their reductionist epistemology. Consequently they have become a scholastic discourse with no relevance or interest for human beings who yearn for holistic experience.

Consideration of divine beauty as understood by the Christian tradition is crucial in our contemporary search for a new spirituality. If we attempt to weave the strands of a new

spirituality around formal theological concepts, we may not
advance much, because that spirituality might turn out to be
another discourse falling into the same trap as any academic
theology. Any emerging spirituality will have to renounce a
monological theology and receive power from both apophatic
silence and economic speech through the medium of beauty.
Experiencing the material reality as beautiful and good is the
key to this medium. This would obviously require a rethinking
of the conceptual and linguistic tools we use in our theology,
though the main thrust of a new spirituality will be in the
experience of the beautiful and "the creativity of the good".[27]
There is again an eclipse of language at the higher levels of this
aesthetic experience. The physical, incarnate reality of Christ as
the self-emptying image of God constitutes the source of beauty
and goodness. The incarnate Christ undergoes the experience of
transfiguration rendering matter luminous and transparent. All
sensible beauty must necessarily pass through this experience in
order "to be initiated into the mystery of the future". The
eschatological dimension of reality is very often equated with
the apocalyptic, with all its dramatic and catastrophic happen-
ings. Christian eschatology has to be seen in the light of a new
aesthetic vision. The final judgment is a discernment of beauty.
The Christian tradition has seen beauty and holiness as identical
and the "image" of God as key to both. This image in us by its
very nature calls us to undertake a pilgrimage to the source of
beauty and holiness in God.

* * *

In this chapter we have tried to point out that theology has
three constitutive dimensions, which interpenetrate each other
dynamically. Christian theology arising out of the incarnation of
the Son of God is sustained by those interdependent dimensions
of human experience in relation to God. Theology thus cannot
be simply monological, taking only human logos as its basis and
means. It cannot be said to be three-dimensional either, because
all the three dimensions we mentioned transcend themselves or
deny themselves in a kenotic movement to open up to the
infinity of God's life and light. A multidimensional theology
has implications for a spirituality of our times. As all good

24

theology follows the experiential itinerary of the incarnate God, so does a sane Christian spirituality. We turn now to some aspects of the image of God as the key to this pilgrimage.

NOTES

[1] Dorothee Sölle, *Thinking About God*, London, SCM Press, 1990, p.1.
[2] R. Panikkar, "Indian Theology: A Theological Mutation", in M. Amaladoss et al., eds, *Theologizing in India*, Bangalore, Theological Publications in India, 1981, p.32.
[3] *Ibid.*, p.34.
[4] Masao Abe, "Kenotic God and Dynamic Sunyata", in John B. Cobb and C. Ives, eds, *The Emptying God*, Maryknoll, NY, Orbis, 1990.
[5] *Ibid.*, p.10.
[6] Quoted by K. Ware, *The Orthodox Way*, London, Mowbray, 1979, pp.30-31.
[7] *Oration* 28.3.
[8] *Ibid.*
[9] Clement of Alexandria, *Paedagogus*, I,5.23.1.
[10] *Oration* 30.3.
[11] *Poems* XI. 113-114.
[12] Athanasius of Alexandria, *Letter to Serapion*, I.28-31.
[13] Benedicta Ward, tr., *The Sayings of the Desert Fathers*, Oxford, Mowbray, 1975, p.69.
[14] *Ibid.*, p.ix.
[15] *Oration* 30.17.
[16] *Op. cit.*, p.37.
[17] *Oration* 29.4.
[18] Gregory of Nazianzus, *Oration*, 28.12.
[19] Sallie McFague, *Models of God*, London, SCM Press, 1987, p.32.
[20] V. Lossky, *The Mystical Theology of the Eastern Church*, London, James Clarke, 1957, p.42.
[21] *Poems* I.1, 29.
[22] *Oration* 29.19.
[23] Jürgen Moltmann, *Le Seigneur de la Danse: Essai sur la joie d'être libre*, tr. A. Liefooghe, Tours, Le Cerf-Marne, 1972, p.82.
[24] P. Evdokimov, *L'art de l'icône*, Paris, Desclee de Brouwer, 1972, p.80.
[25] Paulos Gregorios, *The Human Presence: An Orthodox View of Nature*, Geneva, WCC, 1978, pp.90f.
[26] Patrick Sherry, *Spirit and Beauty: An Introduction to Theological Aesthetics*, Oxford University Press, 1992, p.177.
[27] Paulos Gregorios, *Cosmic Man: The Divine Presence*, New Delhi, Kottayam, Sophia Publications, 1980, p.150.

2. The Self-Effacing Image

Two of the key ideas that have shaped traditional Christian anthropology are the Greek notion of *logos* as human rationality and the Hebraic understanding of the image of God in the human being. Both notions have been used as marks of exclusivity to single out the human species from the rest of living beings and the "inanimate" creation. Then, depending on the social, economic and cultural contexts, these notions have been and are still being used by the dominant powers within the human species to discriminate some human beings from other human beings on the basis of gender, race, intellectual attainment, economic success and so on. Using the ideas of *logos* and *imago Dei* for exclusivist purposes entails a logical chain that can be extended to any area of existence, from justifying a fascist or apartheid regime to exploding the moon in order to alter climatic conditions on earth. The progressive reductionism implicit in this logical chain can appear in various forms in our secular scientific culture and can masquerade as a Christian concept while undermining the original Christian perceptions.

We have seen how our understanding of the deity plays a key role in the case of God-language. So, too, we must review some of our assumptions about our own environment by looking afresh at the decisive notions of logos or human rationality and the image of God as supreme gifts to humanity. The ecological crisis has brought the theological issues underlying these notions to a sharp focus. Any emerging spirituality will have to reckon with these issues.

Much of our contemporary concern for ecology springs from the fear of an impending threat to human life on earth. Basically it reflects the instinct for self-preservation, though it often expresses itself in a romantic embrace of nature or a holistic concern for the integrity of creation. At best, it is enlightened self-interest.

Recent studies have revealed that if human beings try to escape the threat of annihilation only for themselves, without any regard for the rest of creation, they will not succeed. Secular humanistic thinking and scientific-technological progress have come under severe attack for their narrow vision of human well-being at the expense of the rest of creation. Investigations into the human ecosystem from various angles have confirmed the interrelatedness of life on earth and the absolute dependence of the human species on its environment. Insights from experiments in nuclear physics and molecular biology have also helped us to shape the picture of a universe held together by complex and dynamic bonds of mutual relationship. The organic, interrelated nature of the sub-atomic universe as perceived by contemporary physics is being followed up by many environmental philosophers in their own perception of reality. Ecology seems to have become the trend-setter in all fields of human thinking. Theology has followed the trend, as it always does, and begins to speak of the integrity of creation, the theology of creation, the organic relationship within creation and so on.

A new perceptual threshold

The ecological movement in its more rhapsodic and holistic expressions is turning against the main thrust of the dominant secular-scientific worldview which is held in such high esteem in the bastions of Western civilization and its offshoots in the rest of the world. It is advocating, as we see in "deep ecology" for instance, the slowing down or even reversal of a process of progress set in motion by the European Renaissance and re-inforced by colonial conquests and industrial-technological civilization. This, however, is still a rather peripheral move-ment, as "ecology" is being controlled mainly by technocrats, corporate business leaders and politicians, who believe in the primacy of human self-interest and profit-making over against any concern for non-human species or the totality of creation. For them ecological concern seems to represent at best the control and maintenance of the environment in such a way that we can continue to make profit and use the rest of creation for our pleasure. Sustainability is still a human self-oriented notion, though sustainable economics, unlike traditional economics, includes future generations of human beings when it poses its basic question of how to produce what for whom. It also asks the question of conserving irreplaceable resources like water, air, soil, fish and wildlife.[1]

In spite of the many ecological *cris du coeur*, there has so far been no radically effective questioning of the assumptions of the industrial-technological civilization. We cannot assume in a simplistic way that the hard-core believers in progress who control the world scene will soon realize the need for a radical rethinking. It is depressing to think that only some major ecological catastrophe, something far worse than Chernobyl, might induce a higher awareness that can help us cross a new "perceptual threshold" in favour of life on earth. Many people are now turning to humanity's spiritual resources, to ancient traditions of wisdom, in a frantic search for an antidote to the disintegrating trends revealed by the ecological crisis. Christian theology, in coming to terms with the new trends in ecological thinking, has shown signs of its readiness to take a fresh look at some of its own assumptions.

The artist's vision

The Genesis story of the creation of the human being out of the earth signifies an act of differentiating the human being from the rest of creation. Adam begins to acquire a distinct personality as "he" is carved out of the material mass and stamped with the image of God. The process of individuation is not complete with the first human being, as "he" is still in the making. Only when that first human being is further divided into two distinct sexes in the creation of Eve do we see clearly a human man and a human woman. In this sense the first figure of Adam is a common source bearing the image of God for masculine and feminine individuals.

Every artist who creates images knows that this act of differentiation is essential to the art of image-making. Acknowledging that the process of making images is the process of division, the Indian Christian artist Jyoti Sahi points out that the Indo-European concept of "measuring out" is fundamental to the ancient Indian understanding of creation. So important is this in Hindu thought that the artist who wants to create the wholeness of the image begins by dividing the spaces, which is the primary act of composition.[2] Sahi finds a parallel in the creation myth of Genesis where God divides the night from the day, earth from water, woman from man and so on.

It should be assumed that this process of individuation is extended to every part of the universe. When Adam names the animals, he cooperates with the creator in identifying and naming every component of creation. When the physicist discovers and names new particles and forces in the physical universe, it is essentially the same activity. In the mind of the artist, however, this act of differentiation is simply the primary act of composition, that is, bringing together various apparently disjointed elements to create a meaningful whole. The whole picture is present in the mind of the artist while shaping its components, and it is the vision of the whole that provides the artist's creative impulse. It is not surprising that in many ancient cultures the creator of the universe is seen as a supreme artist. In the Genesis account of creation, God's act of shaping the human being out of the clay is obviously an act of the artist. When theologians and exegetes who lack the perceptive *in-sight* of the artist interpret the creation narrative, they may lose sight of the composition of the whole and consequently project the human being out of its context and miss all sense of the interrelatedness and inner harmony of the composition. With increasing emphasis on the reason-based hierarchy of creation and the predominance of the rational dimension in the human person, Christian anthropology began to lose the refreshing and profound insights of the artist into the human mystery.

The total composition is more than the sum of its parts. It transcends logical categories and assumes a meaning that defies verbal explication. Just as every piece of good art has an ineffable dimension that surpasses the critic's attempt to reduce it to a meaningful logical discourse, so creation in its totality stretches out beyond the threshold of rational intelligibility. Humanity and all the rest of creation find their place in the total composition in relation to their orientation to this unuttered dimension.

In considering artistic activity as participation in God's creativity, we need to understand art not as imitation but as creation. The work of even a skilful imitator of a piece of art remains exterior to the mind of its original creator. A true act of creation transposes the artist to the experience of fullness where every fragmentation is overcome and where "fullness remains even when fullness is taken away".[3] Comparing Western notions of art, both classical and Renaissance, with the perception of ancient Chinese art, Simon Leys says that the former, which sees art as possessing an essentially illusionist character, is diametrically opposed to the Chinese idea of the operative power of art on reality.[4] While Western artists believed in the *trompe l'oeil* and measured their success in their ability to fake reality, the norm for Chinese painters was the capacity to summon reality. The painting had an almost magical power over nature. Leys cites two ancient Chinese anecdotes: A horse from the emperor's stable began to limp after Han Gan had painted its portrait. Later it was discovered that the master artist had forgotten to paint one of its hooves. Another story points out the consequence of Wu Daozi's painting of a waterfall on the wall of the imperial palace. The emperor later asked the artist to wipe off the painting, because noise from the waterfall was disturbing his sleep at night!

Tools of alienation

The fruitfulness of the artistic insight for a sane theology of creation may not be apparent in a culture where art itself is reduced to *objets d'art*, possessed and traded by the super rich while artists themselves go hungry. The artist as a perpetual communicator to the roots of being, connecting and composing the whole image in the light of an integral vision, is far from the modern communicator who uses sophisticated electronic means of communication to exploit and alienate God's creation.

Human being as artist differs from human being as maker (*homo faber*). The tool-using maker can stand apart from his or her construction. The making of modern industrial-technological civilization has been the work of *homo faber* who always runs the risk of being alienated from his own creation. It is not cosmic harmony that is the primary goal of the new builder, but immediate physical comfort and the competitive efficiency of production and consumption, regardless of any environmental consequence. This is clearly different from the ancient architectural principles of the construction of a temple or a house with a profound spiritual awareness of cosmic forces and an inclusive sense of the total environment. Like the temple of the deity, human habitat also is a sacred space, built up according to certain spiritual designs that go beyond merely functional considerations.

By instilling his breath and impressing the stamp of his being and love, the artist-creator enters into his very creation. The person of the artist, the tools used and the material worked upon are not ultimately differentiated from one another. The artist can never be alienated from this creation. Similarly, God's loving, self-emptying and sacrificial involvement holds the key to the creation of the world. The Lamb slain from the foundation of the world (Rev. 13:8) is a constant biblical-liturgical theme in Christian tradition. The incarnation of Christ is implicit from the first moment of creation. God as the supreme artist has already entered the creation by compassionate anticipation. Nothing can tear them apart nor objectify the one in isolation from the other. Eastern Christian tradition is quite firm in the conviction that sin has not totally eclipsed the image nor negated the creation as damned. For Christian theology this is confirmed by the incarnation, death and resurrection of Christ. The created nature fully assumed by the incarnate Son cannot be dissociated from Godhead. The glorified Christ continues the great intercession as the incarnate, fully divine and human Christ. The eucharistic celebration is the celebration of the salvation of creation, which is called to transfiguration and deification by the indwelling Spirit.

It is mainly with the rise of modern mechanistic worldviews that God has been spatially relegated to the "up there", only to be declared a non-entity by later, more "enlightened" scientific thinking. A sane Christian tradition can recognize a certain co-inherence of the radical transcendence of God and God's compassionate divine immanence in creation without necessarily postulating logical polarities. This is at the heart of the gospel of the incarnate Christ. The mystery of the incarnate Christ is also the mystery of creation, which acts as a locus for this co-inherent view, essentially a view of the artist. The theologian who operates mostly at the conceptual level with intellectual tools may run the risk of totally missing the sense of this co-inherent composition. Such a theologian is like the art critic or literary critic who seeks to articulate in a rational discourse the meaning of a piece of art. The art critic runs the risk of missing the real sense of the work of art unless he or she becomes an artist. The theologian who attempts to elucidate the object of study in a theological discourse may face the same problem. In the Eastern Christian vocabulary, the spiritual counterpart of the true artist is the saint. As we can say that the true vocation of the art critic is to become an artist, the true vocation of the theologian is to be a saint. When Evagrius Ponticus defines the theologian as the one who prays ("if you pray, you are a theologian"), he hints at this essential transformation. Just as the artist can penetrate to the core of reality through the act of creation, the saint can perceive the transparency of created reality through compassionate prayer that transfigures our ordinary levels of understanding.

Womb-to-womb communication

One of the most beautiful passages in the Bible is the one that narrates the meeting of Mary and Elizabeth in the hill country of Judaea (Luke 1:39-56). Mary, the young virgin carrying Jesus in her womb, meets Elizabeth, the elderly barren woman carrying the embryonic John. The moment is rich with meaning. The barren woman acknowledges that the babe leaped for joy in her womb when she heard the sound of Mary's greeting. Elizabeth in return blesses the fruit of Mary's womb. The mutual blessing is a joyful act that results from a womb-to-womb communication. The two women are taken by surprise in a moment of creative encounter between hidden sources of life energy within them.

In the tradition of the church Mary is the symbol of humanity. As humanity bearing the true image of God greets the apparently barren world, a movement of life happens, a joyful and vital response in the womb of creation. This is essentially an artist's gesture to call forth life where it is least suspected, out of the apparent barrenness of the inanimate creation.

Homo faber, by contrast, is deeply worried about and disturbed by wombs that carry life. He is threatened and threatens in turn. Destruction of dense forests throbbing with rare forms of life and the annihilation of human life with fatal weapons originate in the same source: the aggressive desire to appropriate the material world for one's own pleasure.

Human rationality as tool

The image of God signifies the possibility for the human self to open up to infinite dimensions. This opening up of the self is essentially an interior pilgrimage to the heart of reality, where everything is interconnected. The pilgrim is invited to wander without hearth or home, without the fire of passion-swayed comforts or the security of intellectual shelters. In a self-emptying search for the true self, the pilgrim discovers the image of God in the transparency of relationship of the whole creation within itself and to its creator. The pilgrim's true self identifies itself with the image of God in the heart of creation. This takes place beyond all human self-consciousness, which continually veils the clarity of vision and breaks the delicate threads of deep connections. The human self is no longer the centre that holds the connections. It is precisely by negating this role that the self discovers itself.

In the history of theological reflection, however, the image of God was often understood as an exclusive possession that set humanity apart from the rest of creation. Every insensitive exultation of the privilege attributed to this possession further alienated the human being from God's creation. The disastrous consequence of this line of thought was the identification of the image of God with the greedy and aggressive outreach of the human ego. Invoking the image of God for every form of human enterprise, often in the name of human creativity, without sufficient discernment is a theological commonplace. Ever since the Crusaders and the conquistadors we have seen this theology of the image of God at work in conquering, possessing and dominating. A major theological debate during the early period of Spanish-Portuguese colonialism in Latin America was about whether the native Indians had a human soul, whether they were really human or just sub-human creatures.[5] Instead of a self-denying search in the interior universe, we see a self-extending mission aggressively conquering and enslaving the physical universe.

Logos understood as human rationality is enlisted as the hallmark and privileged instrument of the image of God. In the light of reason, "man" stands out over against the inferior creation, which becomes the object and field of exploitation. As feminist theologians remind us, women also became part of this inferior mass that can be objectified, manipulated and exploited for the whims of a superior rationality thought to subsist in the male image of God. At best man becomes the centre and focal point of an interlocking universe. At worst he distances himself from the creation and enthrones himself as a demi-god.

In the cultural milieu of medieval Europe, where God's unquestionable authority was manifested in an all-powerful and authoritarian church, the Renaissance liberation of human reason was naturally understood as an emancipation of human beings from the oppressive authority of God and the church. History has shown that the liberation of reason as a reaction to the falsification of the God-image has not only produced good fruits but also resulted in the separation between mind and matter, spirit and body, the cerebral and the emotional. The role of the liberated reason in integrating the human person in the community of created reality has been rather ambiguous.

The immediate consequence of this alienation of human reason from the total environment, both human and non-human, is the instrumentalization of human rationality. Once human reason is thrown in between humanity and the rest of creation as a tool of the former to subdue the latter, the original vocation of humanity as a mediating, reconciling presence is completely defeated. In India there is a widely observed festival period when instruments of physical and intellectual labour are laid to rest in an act of worship (*puja*). Agricultural tools and intellectual tools like pen and paper become part of the *puja* in a spiritual gesture which may wish to eliminate any tool that stands between humanity and nature. The Jewish sabbath has a similar aspect in which human interference with nature is restrained by the principle of rest.[6] Here sabbath signifies the joyful harmony of humanity with nature, a state in which the human person is no longer the tiller who makes use of the earth as an object of activity. Since there is no clear limit imposed on human work in the command to till the earth (Gen. 2:15), the tendency to over-till is possible, especially if it is found to be profitable and gratifying to selfish human desires. Modern technological civilization has illustrated the ecological consequences of this human mania.

The problem of technological development is the inability to distinguish between the ploughshare and the sword, between the human need for energy and the proliferation of nuclear arsenals. Civilization based on the belief in progress sees only the perfect logic of human creativity in this development from need-based simplicity to desire-based profligacy. The very tool of human tilling activity, however, turns against humanity. Nuclear power is a good example of a tool becoming an invincible enemy of the human user. Production of nuclear power, whether for peace or for war, carries with it an almost indestructible element of fatal power against all life on earth.

This is a rather unpleasant truth, and we face a real dilemma here. We are fully aware that it is the invention and efficient use of instruments that made human civilization possible. We distinguish ourselves from the animals on this count, telling ourselves that the human being is a "tool-making animal". But while the animals retain vital links with nature, civilized humanity has moved away from many of its fundamental bonds with nature. The dilemma is that we cannot either deny our ability for tool-making and tool-using, as it has been the mainspring of civilized existence, or simply condone the indiscriminate sharpening of simple tools of life into fatal weapons of death. Who will set the limits and on what basis? The utopian vision that some political-economic order might do this for all humanity is now shattered, at least temporarily.

The pivot of sacrifice

Creation theology in the best of Jewish and Christian sources affirms that it is the power of the goodness, will and love of God that creates and sustains the world. God performs an artist's gesture in fashioning creation and entering it by imparting God's own image and vital breath. There is a pivotal element of sacrifice in this which is universally recognized by all ancient patterns of religious thinking, no matter how different may be their worldviews and understanding of creation. As the ancient Rig Veda aphoristically puts it, "sacrifice is the navel of the universe"[7] (*Ayam yajno bhuvanasya nabhi*). The Jewish kabbalistic understanding of *zimsum* and the Christian understanding of the self-emptying of God in Christ (*kenosis*) reflect the crucial significance of the sacrificial dimension inherent in God's continuing act of creation.[8] The so-called primitive religious worldviews are all grounded in myths of the sacrifice of the primordial generative power, whether that be an earth mother or a cosmic father, for the well-being of the world. Here again it can be compared to an artist's gesture of sacrificial self-emptying in the fulfilment of his or her creation.

The elimination of the element of sacrifice from our modern notion of human well-being distorts human creativity. We have become convinced that the vocation of free and creative human beings is to eliminate all pain and suffering from the world. The progress of medicine and other sciences was originally motivated by this enlightened view of human well-being. In our increasing awareness of human rights and freedom this is again intensely reflected. Since the affirmation of this vocation is so essential and integral to a sane anthropology, one is virtually certain to be misunderstood if one points out that the element of sacrifice remains vital for the harmony and wholeness of creation.

The paradox of our search for human dignity and well-being is that it is so subject to a certain cultural model and its political-economic structures that only a very small fraction of humanity can enjoy the fruits of freedom and creativity as proposed by that culture. So imperious is the imposition of this cultural model of well-being that vast millions of the world are deprived of the right to articulate their own models of freedom and creativity, let alone their capacity for economic and political decision-making. This cultural model does not recognize the right to suffer, even the fundamental right of a loving mother to suffer for her children, if we take seriously some of the affirmations of radical feminist theology. No Christian theology would stand firm if we eliminate from it God's self-emptying suffering for the creation, God's very right to suffer. Consequently no anthropology would merit the name Christian if it eliminated the human right to suffer as integral to full humanity. The only difference is that one has no right to impose this suffering on any human being other than one's own self. The idea of human domination over the creation has somehow always tended to eliminate human suffering at the expense of the rest of creation. As this tendency, armed with the weapons of technology, assumes an exclusively hedonistic vocation in our times at the systematic and fatal expense of creation, all life on earth is really threatened.

The frontier role of humanity

Many Christians in the West who despise their own heritage turn desperately to the Oriental wisdom of the Taoist, Buddhist and Hindu traditions for a sane ecological worldview, perhaps without realizing that the Eastern tradition within Christianity has produced a Christian wisdom capable of entering into a sympathetic and fruitful dialogue with both the Oriental philosophical-spiritual worldviews and the secular scientific-technological culture at the same time. Since the Eastern Christian tradition never conformed to nor approved the colonial model of expansionist, conquering and owning mission, it was ignored as less than Christian by Western Christians in general. The Christian Orient shares much common ground with Oriental non-Christian religious worldviews in its insights into the nature of reality. These insights are synthesized by the genius of Eastern Christian spirituality on the basis of theological presuppositions different from those prevalent in the West, especially since Augustine of Hippo.

A remarkable contemporary attempt to elucidate the holistic Eastern Christian perception of reality in dialogue with secular scientific culture and with Oriental religious-philosophical traditions is seen in the work of Metropolitan Gregorios. Basing himself on the thought of St Gregory of Nyssa (330-395), one of the most profound Christian thinkers of all time, Gregorios brings out the mediating role of human presence in creation. His writings show clearly that an exploitatively domineering figure of the human being over against nature is certainly not the heart of Eastern Christian anthropology. Humanity as the mediator (*methorios*) or the frontier being that mediates between the material and the spiritual, between the secular and the sacred, between God and creation has a quite different vocation.

Gregory of Nyssa and his fellow Eastern theologians did attribute a royal character to humanity and underlined the dominion of human nature over the rest of creation by virtue of human freedom. However, this freedom has to be exercised in the control of will and the practice of love and justice. This idea of freedom as the hallmark of the image of God in humanity has nothing to do with the Augustinian tradition in the West, which assumed a rather pessimistic view, pointing to the power of sin over human nature, which is deprived of the freedom even to will good. "Image of God means participation in the very characteristics of God — to be the perfection of all good, all beauty, all love, all wisdom, all power. This, rather than sin, as in Augustine, is the decisive and distinctive element in man."[9]

One of the problems of the great Oriental religio-philosophical systems is their neglect of the human person within a sweepingly cosmic holism. The social-ethical implications of this attitude for human dignity, justice, equality and freedom are obvious. The Eastern Christian tradition has been particularly aware of this. It was also aware of the other pole, in which self-alienated human rationality holds sway and enthrones itself as the unique instrument in the interpretation of reality. So the image of God in humanity is seen not in terms of a domineering and despotic figure over against creation, but in human self-discipline, justice, freedom and above all love. As Metropolitan Gregorios explains it:

> We best see the royal stature of man in those who have really become free by learning to control their own wills. When man wears the purple of virtue and the crown of justice, he becomes a living image of the king of kings, of God himself. The beauty of God is the beauty of joy, of beatitude, of blessedness. God is love, and when love is absent in man, his image disappears. [10]

This insight may be developed in various ways:

1. The image as corporate:

Humanity together with the material creation constitutes the ultimate image of God. Most modern theological discussion on the image of God is confined to the relation between God and the individual human being. This is still further restricted to the individual's inner qualities like intelligence, will and rationality. The body of the individual and corporate humanity tend to be neglected. Creation as a whole is not made a serious partner in the reflection.

Creation in all its complexity is assigned its legitimate role in a sane reflection on the God-world-humanity relationship. Such reflection is rooted in a remarkably positive view of created reality as the expression of God's goodness, love and will and in the truth of the incarnation of Christ, who is the archetype for the mediatory presence of humanity between spirit and matter, God and creation. The integral connection between God, creation, incarnation and humanity is so overwhelmingly present in the concept of humanity as a frontier being that dichotomies are eliminated.

Discussion of the so-called "anthropic principle"[11] — whether the physical properties of matter and the universe were made to fit life or whether life evolved to fit the physical environment — may not be very fruitful in the light of a holistic vision in which both the evolution of matter and the evolution of life are rooted together in the same source of being and therefore reflect deep ontological interconnections between them. Biological and cosmological evolutions are sustained and interwoven by ontological involutions that constantly connect every particle of the universe among them and to the original source from which they spring in such a way that the continuous and symphonic unfolding of creation happens. This process of unfolding cannot be reduced to a simple linear historical scheme. On the contrary, our awareness of linear history of past, present and future is only an aspect of the rich and complex spectrum of the unfolding of created reality.

The hesitation in certain circles of Christian theology to consider the human body and through it the material creation as constitutive of the image of God may be due to a fear of falling into an anthropomorphic concept of God. So the image of God is understood in terms of exclusively non-material and psychological qualities. This tendency, however, ignores the fact that a human being is rooted in matter just as a tree is rooted in earth, though in a different mode. It is the bodiliness of the human person that provides the roots and sustains the image in its wholeness. The modern celebration of the cerebral has neglected these roots. The obvious reaction to this neglect has been visible in the cult of the body and its passions.

The idea that by virtue of the image of God, human beings are carved out and set apart in creation, whether through their erect physical stature, freedom or rationality, can easily be abused. It has effectively been abused by setting the human being over against creation, making creation an object of selfishly exercised human freedom and creating divisions of superiority and inferiority between different races of human beings and between sexes. The claim of humanity to bear the image of God must be set within the human vocation of discovering the larger and deeper dimension of the image in the totality of creation. This is no idolizing of material entities in the world, but a rediscovery of the one *corpus* (body) of creation, of which humanity is a constitutive member. An *oikosomatic* model of reality, in which the material creation becomes "my Father's house" (*oikos*) and "my body" (*soma*), may also help the rediscovery of the larger dimension of the image. [12]

In the light of the mediation between the spiritual and the material by humanity, all "human" decisions are to be made in consultation with nature and the creation at large. The apparently simple act of cutting a tree must no longer be a purely unilateral human decision. Creation, as it has been stamped with the seal of God's love, free will and goodness, has to be an active participant in all human exercise of will and freedom, so that it may actively contribute to the creativity of love and goodness. Dietary regulations in major religions, prayer, fasting and acts of compassion, if understood rightly, are all various modes of "consulting God's creation" in the ongoing decision-making processes of life. In the prayers of the Christian tradition, we usually ask forgiveness of other human beings, not of all other living beings. But in some Asian traditions, like the Jain religion of India, which is the source of the famous principle of *ahimsa* or non-violence popularized in the political practice of Mahatma Gandhi, daily confession of even the minutest acts of violence is followed by the scriptural prayer of pardon addressed to all living beings: "I ask pardon of all living beings. May they forgive me. May I remain in friendship with all beings and have enmity with none." [13]

This kind of asking pardon is another way of consulting God's creation. Human life is understood not in terms of an exclusivist autonomy and individual freedom which alienate humanity from the rest of creation, but in the light of a universal *compassion* which presupposes the organic interconnection of a household and a body. Even the sometimes caricatured Islamic practice of saying *bismillah* ("in the name of God") while slaughtering animals for food shows that life is being taken just for the purpose of providing the essential human need for food.

The Cappadocian Fathers called human body and matter in general *homodoulos* ("fellow servant") of the spirit. In their understanding both spirit and matter are joined in the creation of the human being so that both together may aspire to be divinized. In the great pilgrimage of creation, the spirit leads the body as a co-pilgrim and fellow-seeker. Since the union of spirit and body is effected in the original creation, matter and material creation cannot be extricated from its vocation of transfiguration and divinization. The incarnation of Christ and the transfiguration of the body he assumed from the womb of creation cannot be understood in isolation from the original vocation of created material reality. As Kallistos Ware says:

> Man is not saved from his body but in it; not saved from the material world but with it. Because man is microcosm and mediator of the creation, his own salvation involves also the reconciliation and transfiguration of the whole animate and inanimate creation around him — its deliverance "from the bondage of corruption" and entry "into the glorious liberty of the children of God" (Rom. 8:21). In the "new earth" of the Age to come there is surely a place not only for man but for the animals: in and through man, they too will share in immortality, and so will rocks, trees and plants, fire and water. [14]

The image of God, beginning with the original union, pervades the entire breadth and depth of this complex reality. The image of God can be "located" at every point where spirit touches matter. There is no point in creation where matter does not touch the spirit. If human bodies are holy because they are temples of the Holy Spirit, creation is also holy because of the same indwelling Spirit in it. This is not a passive, pantheistic experience, because human freedom can act together with the Spirit in perfecting and realizing this holiness.

2. The image as open-ended:

Image is continually in the making. Humanity becomes in a special way the locus where the creation makes its continual *epiclesis* or calling upon the Spirit. We constantly call upon the Spirit who is already present with us and in us. There is nothing fixed and already past here. The very being of creation depends on being in continuous give-and-take with the Spirit, expressed in the ecclesial act of the invocation of the Spirit. The church as a community does the invocation on behalf of all creation. If there is no *epiclesis*, there is no church. God in his ineffable wisdom must have provided the creation with various means unknown to us of doing this invocation. However, we as human beings and as Christians belonging to the great community of faith across time and space undertake to do it on behalf of all creation within our limited knowledge of reality. This is done in an attitude of reverence for the mystery of creation, and not in a condescending spirit.

Epiclesis is at the same time an act of both image-making and image-breaking. It is an act of image-making, or being shaped in the image of God, because the image of God is a seal and a promise to be realized in the process of uniting the spiritual and the material creation and initiating it into the infinite possibilities of life in God. Humanity alone is not the actor nor the acted-upon. In a synergistic togetherness with the Spirit of God and the incarnate Christ, both humanity and the whole creation together shape and are shaped in the image of God.

Epiclesis is also an act of image-breaking, because humanity has the option of using its freedom to make false images. Human self and human concepts can stand as opaque images between God and creation. Humanity becomes the locus for the invocation of the Spirit precisely because it can turn out to be the locus where the power of evil continually threatens to encamp. So the breaking of false images and the elimination of their power constitute the other side of making or being made in the image of God.

Within our limited knowledge of reality, we can affirm that justice, freedom and dignity — not only for human beings, but for all living beings — are signs, though modest and partial, of the process of creative image-making. When the major part of humanity is subject to conditions of misery, bondage and indignity and when nature is ravaged and many species of living beings are annihilated by human greed, we cannot possibly be complacent about the image of God once and for all given to humanity.

3. The image as self-effacing:

In the Christian tradition, we rightly uphold every human person as a unique bearer of the image of God. This does not however justify the individualistic interpretation of the image as a possession of an individual or group of individuals over against the rest of creation. When it is understood as a possession and when reason is highlighted as the core of that possession, we are implicitly constructing a hierarchy — male/female and human/non-human — with its endless ramifications in the descending order of value and importance. If this hierarchy turns out to be exploitative and oppressive, as some radical feminists and deep ecologists have observed, the source of the "image of God" is no longer the creator God, but some human beings or structures who project their own self onto other human beings and onto the material world. Everything becomes a possession, an extension of the ego.

In the history of the modern world, especially since the beginning of colonial conquests, the construction of reality is centred on the image of man as explorer, conqueror and owner. Western theology in a very triumphalist manner lent its hierarchy-based theology of the image of God to the self-image of the conquistadors in political and missionary conquests. Unknown physical and intellectual space was to be explored in order to conquer and own.

This was true in political colonial expansion, in missionary enterprises and in the explorations of science and technology. An image of the human being, inflated with cultural, racial and religious hubris, drove the conquistador, the missionary and the scientist to enterprises that aimed at possession and mastery of the universe. The 500th anniversary of the "discovery of America" by Christopher Columbus in 1992 was a sad occasion to be reminded of all holocausts — cultural, racial, intellectual and religious — committed by the new "master and possessor of nature" in the name of a "modern, civilized, Christian" self-image of the human being. It was also a reminder that modern industrial-technological civilization continues to believe that all available space in the universe is for the free (that is, indiscriminate) use of human beings. Whether it is outer space or the depths of the sea or the polar regions, humanity makes a claim on it on the basis of decisions taken by certain human beings out of narrow political or economic self-interest.

In traditional worldviews physical space is allocated not only for human beings but also for spirits and divine powers. Temples and shrines are sacred spaces set apart as spirit domains. One can say that in these worldviews there is a recognition of "spirit rights" similar to our modern awareness of "human rights". During the seventh assembly of the World Council of Churches (Canberra 1991), Chung Hyun-Kyung, the

Korean Presbyterian professor of theology, shocked many people by her dramatic invocation of all spirits, including those of sea animals and various non-human species exterminated by human greed. She threw off her shoes on stage declaring the ground a sacred space. It would not be unfair to interpret this as a protest by the Korean Presbyterian theologian against her own Christian heritage, the Western Reformation tradition, imported into Korea, which suppressed important elements of ancient Korean culture by the suppression of spirit rights and the sense of sacred space in the name of an "enlightened" Christian understanding of the world. One could also interpret that extreme reaction in Freudian terms, the Oedipal killing of the father-image of a self-imposing, paternalistic Western culture and the marrying of the traditional mother culture by the child come of age. [15] The Western "enlightened" version of the gospel preached to the Asians never took seriously the complex religious cultural world of the ancient peoples of Asia. Sacred space and spirit rights deeply rooted in the Asian psyche were ruthlessly suppressed or brushed aside by the greedy colonial master of the earth.

Elimination of all sacred space goes hand in hand with the secularizing notion that the universe explored and owned by reason is identical with reality itself. Exploration and exploitation of all unknown space is the extension of human rationality as the privileged instrument of the image of God in the human being. Conversion of the "pagans" who lived outside the borders of the rational universe of the enlightened West meant the appropriation and logical ordering of the still irrational elements of the universe by the real owner and their integration to its logical universe. The same assumptions motivated the colonial conquests and the progress of science since the European renaissance. No wonder that all living beings except a privileged group of humans lost much of their physical space as well as their inner space of self-respect and dignity, and became the exploited victims of an arrogant *imago Dei*.

The human vocation of naming the created beings (Gen. 2:19) is often confused with this exploring and possessing activity. The latter is often called human creativity. Everything that is named becomes automatically the property of the one who names it. What Metropolitan Gregorios calls the "creativity of the good" is the true Christian interpretation of the naming activity and is just the opposite of this form of naming in order to own. It is not possessing, but nurturing the good, an activity that always fosters life, an exercise of freedom that works together with the creative spirit of God.

Understanding the image of God as a privilege and possession of the individual engenders the awareness of the self and the urge to possess. The true Christian spiritual tradition emphasizes the self-emptying and dispossessing dimension of our life as the space of freedom for all creation. It is an act of creative "de-naming", in silence, in compassion, fully respecting the mystery of creation. Freedom exercised with universal compassion is the antidote for the misuse of freedom and rationality understood as individual human privilege.

It is only by self-limiting that humanity can provide living space for the rest of creation. This is primarily a spiritual act with ethical implications, not necessarily a physical act of reducing the biological volume of humanity. It is not always the most populous nations that appropriate space at the fatal expense of other created beings, but often the powerful ones which are numerically much smaller. It is only by discovering the vital connection between the image of God in corporate humanity and God's self-emptying act of incarnation in Christ that we can restore the lost balance of the vision of creation in our times. The paradox of Christ making the whole creation his *body* by the kenotic act of *dispossessing* the self sets the paradigm for a Christian approach to creation.

NOTES

[1] William Chandler, "Designing Sustainable Economies", in L.R. Brown, et al., eds, *State of the World*, New York, W.W. Norton, 1987.
[2] Jyoti Sahi, *The Child and the Serpent: Reflections on Popular Indian Symbols*, London, Routlege and Kegan Paul, 1980, pp.25-26.
[3] *Brihadarnyaka Upanishad*, V, 1.
[4] Simon Leys, *The Burning Forest*, London, Paladin, 1985, pp.29-31.
[5] H. McKennie Goodpasture ed., *History of Christianity in Latin America*, Maryknoll, NY, Orbis, 1989, p.23. The assessment was so negative that Pope Paul III had to declare in a bull of 1536 that native Indians were fully human and should not be barred from eucharist.
[6] Erich Fromm, *You Shall Be As Gods*, New York, Fawcett, 1966, p.154.

[7] *Rig Veda*, I, 164, 35.

[8] For a Christian theological interpretation, see Jürgen Moltmann, *God in Creation: An Ecological Doctrine of Creation*, London, SCM Press, 1985, pp.86ff.

[9] Paulos Mar Gregorios, *Cosmic Man: The Divine Presence*, New York, Paragon, 1988, p.138.

[10] Paulos Mar Gregorios, *The Human Presence: An Orthodox View of Nature*, Geneva, WCC, 1978, p.70.

[11] Charles Birch, *On Purpose*, Kensington, New South Wales University Press, 1990, pp.70,122.

[12] K.M. George, "Towards a Eucharistic Ecology", in G. Limouris, ed., *Justice, Peace and Integrity of Creation: Insights from Orthodoxy*, Geneva, WCC, 1990, pp.45-55.

[13] *Pratikramana-Sutra*, 49.

[14] Kallistos Ware.

[15] K.M. George, "Gospel, Culture and Theological Education", in *The Ecumenical Review*, Vol. XLIII, no. 4, October 1991, pp.459-64.

3. The Stranger's Hospitality

The metaphor of the pilgrim and pilgrimage is at the heart of Christian spirituality. Even in those streams of Reformation tradition which condemned and abolished literal pilgrimages to holy places because of obvious abuses in mediaeval practice, the metaphor re-emerges in contemporary theological reflection with a focus on the eschatological character of the church.

One of the most powerful features of early Christianity was its deep sense of the transitoriness of the present age and its eager waiting for the age to come. "Here we have no lasting city, but we are looking for the city that is to come" (Heb. 13:14). We are only pilgrims on the way to "the Jerusalem above; she is free, and she is our mother" (Gal. 4:25-26). The vision of a new heaven and a new earth symbolized by "the holy city, the new Jerusalem, coming down out of heaven from God" (Rev. 21:1-2) kept the hope aflame in the hearts of the pilgrims amidst earthly trials and persecutions. The New Testament hope for the heavenly Jerusalem, the city that is to come, has to be understood against the obligation prescribed in the Torah for all Jewish males "to go up" to Jerusalem three times a year for the three festivals of Passover, Weeks and Tabernacles. These pilgrimages were integral to Jewish faith and practice.

Around the turn of the first Christian century, Clement, bishop of the young church of Rome, reflecting the prevailing mood of the early church, began his famous letter to the church in Corinth thus: "The church of God which resides as a stranger at Rome to the church of God which is a stranger at Corinth."[1] The word for stranger (*paroikos*) can also stand for pilgrim, sojourner and exile. The word "parish" (*paroikia*), a community of pilgrims or sojourners, has the same origin, though today it conveys to us a well-established and highly organized local Christian community.

One second-century Christian document, drawing on Platonic notions of body and soul, stated:

> Christians dwell in their own countries, but simply as sojourners. As Christians they share in all things with others, and yet endure all things as if foreigners. Every foreign land is to them as their mother country and every land of their birth as a land of strangers.[2]

The figures of the pilgrim and the stranger evoked a profound sense of detachment, non-possession, continuous movement and homelessness. Their impact on Christian spirituality took widely diverse forms, from radical prophetic and revolutionary criticism of society to highly pietistic practices. In the metaphor of pilgrimage, what is of interest to many theologians is the journey itself and not the destination. Referring to the ascent of Moses to the presence of Yahweh on Mount Sinai, Gregory of Nyssa suggests that the spiritual journey is, in fact, a continuous and never ending ascent (*anabasis*). One who travels into the infinity of God's nature cannot possibly think of an end. One never reaches the summit, but climbs on without stopping or turning back. In the Pauline sense, the whole Christian life becomes "a straining forward (*epektasis*) to what lies ahead" (Phil. 3:13).

In the history of the church, radical Christians burning with prophetic zeal for the kingdom of God have often deplored the failure of institutional Christianity to recall that Jesus lived the life of a wanderer and a pilgrim. Born in a manger, rejected by the social structures of security and comfort, Jesus' ministry was pervaded throughout by the sense of homelessness: "Foxes have holes and birds of the air have nests, but the Son of Man has nowhere to lay his head" (Luke 9:58). He gathered his disciples, not into a secure and stable home, but to share in his work of an itinerant preacher of the kingdom to come and a wandering healer of all kinds of sickness.

The movement started by Jesus announced the passing away of the present and the imminent coming of the new age. The peripatetic teacher did not reject the daily world of the people around him, but announced the transformation of the reality of their lives in the light of the incoming kingdom. So healing, the act of restoring and transforming the integrity of bodies, minds and spirits that were subject to the power of disintegration, was central to his ministry. His suffering and death *outside* the city gate was of great symbolic significance for the early church. It evoked a call "to go to him outside the camp and bear the abuse he endured" (Heb. 13:12-13). Many martyrs and prophets have understood this in its profound spiritual sense as a call to set out on pilgrimage, leaving behind the securities of the present age in order to suffer with the outcasts and the marginalized — not a pilgrimage to escape the reality of this world, but a journey to the very heart of that reality in order to transform, sanctify and save it.

The self-emptying of God in the incarnate Christ was God's act of self-exile, the undertaking of a pilgrimage to the heart of created reality. Christ the new Adam, the stranger to the scheme of this world, became the co-traveller with Adam the outcast wandering on the rugged earth and with Cain the murderer, the condemned and solitary wanderer.

Seekers in the desert

The ascetic-monastic tradition of the church tried from the very beginning to assimilate the spirit of the incarnation of Christ and follow the model of the wandering Son of Man who accepted the human condition of being a stranger on earth without home and country. Christ in his incarnate state identified himself with the existential situation of humanity exiled from God's tender love and compassion. As the early Eastern theologians put it, philanthropy or the love for human beings was the divine motivation for incarnation. There is a deep interrelationship between the ascetic-monastic aspiration and God's act of self-emptying. Monastic spirituality, which became paradigmatic for the Eastern Christian tradition and a part of the Western tradition, was tested for truth against its capacity to unveil this relationship in its vision and practice. The flight to the desert, whose purpose was generally understood even by some ascetics as to be "alone with the Alone", did not always capture the true spirit of that move-ment. In those anchorites and monks who *successfully* fought the spiritual combat in the inhospitable aridity of the desert, the struggle produced not a sterile and negative attitude to the world, but a presence full of tenderness, compassion and openness to others. Those human beings who have "over-come the world" were understood to be more compassion-ately committed to the world, though unswayed by its passions — *apatheia*. To be sure, this sort of high spiritual achievement belonged to only a few and not to all who fled to the desert in search of a spiritual oasis. Nevertheless, the ideal and its actual spiritual appropriation even by these few were never understood as purely individual achievements. They constituted the common fund of experience of the Christian community and entered the heart of the tradition of the church at large. It is precisely at this point that monastic spirituality becomes interesting and relevant to our theology and spirituality today.

Very early in the monastic tradition, the theme of *xeniteia,* the state of being a stranger or foreigner (*xenos*) became popular.[3] Leaving one's country of birth, family and possessions and setting off on a journey to a foreign land where one is a total stranger came to be considered the essential starting point for the new spiritual orientation. From the point of view of religious phenomenology, the occurrence of this theme in other world religions and philosophical systems is a commonplace. The Stoic philosopher Epictetus wanted the young aspirants to "leave their brothers, fatherland, friends and family" if they wished to become philosophers. The deeply rooted Hindu and Buddhist image of the mendicant philosopher and itinerant ascetic remains a living tradition, exemplified in the life of *sanyasins* and *bhikshus.*

The pilgrim who accepts voluntary exile is wrested from the cares of daily life, at least temporarily. This is one of the benefits of pilgrimage to the temple, according to the famous first-century Jewish philosopher and theologian Philo of Alexandria. For John Climacus, the famous Christian spiritual writer from the Sinai in the seventh century, *xeniteia* is the leaving behind, without return, of everything at home that obstructs us from pursuing the goal of piety. The monk who abandons hearth and home and all its cares looks for *hesychia*, the deep inner quietness, the true freedom of the soul.

The way of the pilgrim was of crucial importance in the monastic tradition. By accepting the path of humiliation and rejection, the monk is trying to follow the spiritual itinerary of Christ himself. In a well-known poem on being a stranger (*al aksenaiutha*), attributed to St Ephrem, the fourth-century Syrian poet, monk and theologian, the monk is portrayed as a vagabond who has no home, country or means and sleeps on bare ground with a stone as pillow, exposed to heat and cold, hunger and thirst. He is constantly subject to insults and humiliation by others and is contemptuously treated as a beggar, thief, spy or insane. This is typically the condition of *xeniteia*, the state of being a stranger on earth, a radical spiritual attempt to share the self-emptying of God in Christ for the sake of love for humanity.

The actual physical journey to a foreign land, which many monks, especially in the Syrian tradition, undertook as essential for their spiritual combat, soon gave way to an interiorized and symbolic understanding of being a stranger, particularly in Egyptian desert spirituality. The monk can stay where he is provided he practises total detachment from everything in his environment that makes him familiar and "at home" in this world. "Remain in your cell" was the regular advice given by spiritual elders to the inexperienced monks tormented by spiritual listlessness or restlessness. Desire to go out physically in search of spiritual goals can be disappointing and a snare of the evil one.

Guillaumont traces the preference of the Syrian monks to take the route as pilgrims and vagabonds to their inherited mercantile instinct, which took them to many Asian countries like China and India as missionaries. The Coptic monks on the other hand were mostly hard-willed Egyptian peasants from the Nile valley and delta, for whom leaving the world simply meant separating themselves from their village and fields and moving into the desert. Once they were in the depth of the desert they had to stick to the rule of remaining in their cells.[4] The famous monastic principle of *stabilitas in peregrinatione*, remaining in one place while travelling — is the interiorization of the ideal of *xeniteia* and an example of the influence of the Oriental monastic tradition on Western monasticism.

Many stories from monastic history illustrate the need of practising unfamiliarity in the most familiar surroundings. *The Sayings of the Desert Fathers,* the famous collection of spiritual sayings and anecdotes from fourth- and fifth-century Egyptian ascetics, both men and women, tells the story of a young monk who came to Abba Agathon in Scetis seeking spiritual advice. "I want to live with the brothers," said the young man. "Tell me how to live with the brothers."

"All the days of your life," counselled the spiritual father, "keep the frame of mind of the stranger which you have on the first day you join them, so as not to become too familiar with them."[5]

In fact, the flight to the desert or travel to a foreign country is not an essential element in the spiritual vocation of a true pilgrim. One can develop a spirituality of exile while living with others. As the spiritual mother (Amma) Syncletica rather sarcastically put it: "There are many who live in the mountains and behave as if they were in the town, and they are wasting their time. It is possible to be a solitary in one's mind while living in a crowd, and it is possible for one who is a solitary to live in the crowd of his own thoughts."[6]

The end of the biblical story of the fall of humanity is also the beginning of a new story, the journey of Adam and his descendants on the face of a rugged and inhospitable earth. Cain the murderer, son of Adam, carries the curse of humanity and wanders aimlessly in a hostile world. Yet he carries the seal of divine compassion, a protection against complete disintegration. Adam and his progeny entered on a cosmic pilgrimage, treading myriads of routes on earth, ever in search of their true home. Christ the second Adam joined them on the way and became a co-traveller.

Abraham, the stranger-host

Abraham is the pilgrim-stranger par excellence. He left his home and country and set off to an unknown land. He abandoned the stability and prosperity he enjoyed in the land of the Chaldeans, the cradle of civilization, and became a homeless nomad, vaguely searching for a home not yet known, simply believing in the promise of God (Gen.12:1). Taking his barren wife along, he crossed barren deserts and stayed in foreign lands while sharing with his wife the pain of sterility.

The journey of Abraham was a favourite subject of allegorical interpretations by both Jewish and Christian theologians. It became a symbol of the spiritual exodus of the soul leaving behind all that is familiar, making the whole life on earth a constant pilgrimage and enduring the hardships and perils of a life in exile in a strange land. As the author of the Letter to the Hebrews interprets it, "By faith he stayed for a time in the land he had been promised, as in a foreign land, living in tents, as did Isaac and Jacob, who were heirs with him of the same promise. For he looked forward to the city that has foundations, whose architect and builder is God" (11:9-10).

While strangers and nomads, Abraham and Sarah hosted the angels of God outside their tent by the oaks of Mamre (Gen. 18). The hospitality of Abraham and Sarah to the three angels became known in Christian theology as the Old Testament pre-figuration of the Holy Trinity. Through the celebrated icon of the fifteenth-century Russian artist Andrei Rublev, the theme of Abraham's hospitality (*philoxenia*, literally "love of the stranger", entered the world of Christian art.

It is significant that Abraham received the strangers *outside* his tent. We have already mentioned how the early church inter-preted the significance of his location for the church's own self-awareness as a community of strangers and sojourners (Heb. 13:12-13), yet offering hospitality to the strangers, who hap-pened to be the angels of God prefiguring the trinitarian mystery.

In the icon of Rublev, the tree representing the oaks of Mamre symbolizes nature, the whole of creation and ultimately the tree of life, which carries the symbolism of the cross and perfect communion with God. Hospitality is offered and received in the lap of nature, making the creation a partner in the act of communion. It is a stranger inviting strangers to rest a while in a particular place outside all human construction, which can shut off space from theophanic experience. The place is rendered holy by the communion of hospitality.

The tree behind the three angelic guests conveys a very discreet yet vivid presence, neither dominantly overshadowing the guests and host nor reduced in perspective to the vanishing point. It is the presence of the kingdom of God in its invisible visibility. It is the cross of Christ and the *axis mundi*, linking and reconciling earth and heaven, creation and creator, material and spiritual into one communion.

It is doubtful whether the hospitality of Abraham, who stands as a common father to the three great Semitic religions, has been given its proper place in the dominant theological traditions of the Christian church. What the world has seen in aggressive missions and colonial conquests, arrogantly abusing the natural hospitality of the peoples of the world and brutally exploiting the earth which is capable of becoming the place of theophanic communion, is definitely the opposite of true Abrahamic hospitality.

More than a metaphor

Many languages use the same word for both guest and host, as in the Latin *hospes* (from which "hospitality" is derived) or the Greek *xenos*, which can denote a stranger who is welcomed or who acts as a welcomer. The double meaning of one who receives and one who is received is significant, since this potential reversal of roles points to the reciprocity of relationship between guest and host. In the liturgical tradition of the church, Christ is qualified as both guest and host, as offerer and receiver at the same time. In most ancient cultures, the hospitable act of sharing food, shelter and exchanging gifts is at the root of ensuring peace and harmony in a chaotic world.

Christian ethical commitment and the concern for justice in a world of poverty and oppression are theologically rooted in the virtue of hospitality. The church's self-understanding as a pilgrim and an exile can help it enormously to be involved in the predicament of all those who are vulnerable and marginalized. The body of Christ follows the experience of Christ as a vagrant on earth, homeless and weak, yet receiving, healing and reconciling the world in the one household of God.

The founding of hospitals, orphanages, leprosoriums and inns for pilgrims and travellers was basically motivated by this Christian view of hospitality to the stranger, the weak and the wretched. To receive them was to receive Christ himself. As the words of Christ in Matthew 25:35-40 make clear, every act of kindness done to any of these people in need, however insignificant, is done to Christ himself. Receiving everyone as if that person were Christ became a fundamental principle for monastic communities in the East and West.

Thomas Ogletree takes hospitality as the over-arching metaphor for dealing with the issue of the other in fundamental ethics: "to be moral is to be hospitable to the stranger".[7] He criticizes the Western tendency to begin and end ethical analysis with a self who interprets and assimilates the experience of the other in terms of its own experience, so that the other becomes an object of one's own life project. Following Paul Ricoeur, he advocates a "decentring of perspective" from the centredness of the self.[8]

He also appeals to Emmanuel Levinas's effort to locate the commencement of moral consciousness in a readiness to welcome the other. The act of welcoming the other judges and calls into question one's own egoism. Though egoism is presupposed in any moral relationship with the other who is separate from me, it can be transformed at a deeper level into a confirmation of selfhood which, paradoxically, is effected in the radical capacity for self-giving to the other without limit.[9]

Ogletree also finds interesting Levinas's insight into the asymmetrical character of the hospitality relationship between the host and the stranger. The stranger, socially and psychologically vulnerable, cannot maintain an equality of power with the host. The stranger needs shelter, recognition and food as well as orientation to an unfamiliar setting. However, as the stranger begins to tell stories, thus opening up a new world for the host and relativizing the absoluteness of the latter's "home", the relationship becomes more balanced. A new kind of asymmetry arises as a new world is unveiled in which the host is a stranger. The host now has to learn from the stranger, who has authority over this new world. This new asymmetry in favour of the stranger counterbalances the initial asymmetry in favour of the host and gradually produces interactions based on equality and reciprocity.

Under conditions of structural inequality, hospitality alone is an insufficient moral response to social oppression, as the host is "at home" and retains control. In such a situation there is virtually no possibility for a reciprocal relationship between host and guest. Condescension and paternalism corrupt hospitable intentions. The host who decides to renounce the particular location which gives power and privilege will also become a victim of the oppressive structures and will no longer have any further recourse than to move in solidarity with the oppressed. The appropriate response to a situation of oppression, then, is not merely hospitality, but repentance, the complete turning away from the familiar world to the possibility of a new order.

In a situation where one part of the world lives in great affluence and the other part in misery, Christian social diakonia runs the risk of becoming a charity show. The mutuality of sharing as both guest and host can be replaced by paternalistic acts of charity which in the long run might alienate the partners from each other rather than bringing them together into the experience of communion.

It should be gratefully acknowledged that in some affluent Northern societies, characterized by xenophobia, many churches have taken a bold stand in favour of immigrants, refugees and exiles, witnessing to the *philoxenia*, the hospitality of God shown to us sinners through the compassionate being of Christ. But it is a matter of continuing concern that the more successful a society becomes in terms of economic and social structures of welfare, the less hospitable it becomes to outsiders, who are identified as sources of instability and disorder. So xenophobia, fear of the stranger, becomes integrated as a positive social value rather understood as a symptom of selfish insularity and rejection of the other.

It is common knowledge that the poor are more willing to share what they have than the rich. The more one possesses, the less inclined one is to share. Hospitality thus reminds us of our basic call to be pilgrims and strangers and to maintain a sense of detachment towards possessions. It points to the freedom of the human person whose dignity does not depend on material possessions. True sharing and communion between human beings become possible only if they can experience this freedom.

Societies which provide their members a high degree of economic security will also increasingly restrict the space for fools, for the insane, for vagrants and mendicants. All forms of vagabondage are suspect. Although no one would question that such measures of restriction are motivated by concern for the welfare of all, they may eliminate the spiritual potential for dispossession and self-denial which is essential for a new world order. Some rare individuals who voluntarily accept to be in such categories out of prophetic compassion for the world can open up the radical meaning of hospitality to the rest of society. The counter-culture movement powerfully, though rather negatively, brought to light that the human spirit also needs the way of the vagrant, the search for transcendence, beyond the secure settlements of civilization.

Hospitality in its cosmic dimension breaks open the closed world of human societies. If the space for hospitality is constitutive of a household, it implies a perpetual opening of that household to the world outside, fervent hope for the promises of future and joyful anticipation of the other in the midst of one's family.

In traditional non-industrialized societies, children are the most joyful at the coming of guests and visitors, who often arrive without notice. For children, the unexpected presence of free-loading vagrants, mendicants who visit at regular intervals, passing pilgrims who stay for a while and aimless eccentrics opens up an exciting new world. Children sit around and listen to the incredible stories they tell. A sense of mystery surrounds most of these visitors, and the enigma of the worlds they represent remains deep within the hearts of children.

Cosmic hospitality

Hospitality in its cosmic dimension presupposes an order of relationship that transcends the predominant cultural constructions of reality based on subject-object duality and rational-propositional paradigms. In the evolution of human language within a framework of increasing polarization between mind and matter, between myself and the other, the primal perception of designating both guest and host by a single sign has been eclipsed. Projecting human ego as the measure of all onto the complex grid of creation has resulted in a closure of reality rather than a creative disclosure of its own inner resources.

The observation that living organisms are open systems, existing in states of non-equilibrium and contingent on vital elements external to themselves, signifies some sort of constitutive hospitality operating in creation. The sharing of air and earth, sun and space, fire and water by all organisms in common is not just eco-poetry or some ancient philosophical speculation on co-breathing (the *sympnoia* of the Stoics), but the actual physical-biological communion experienced by creation. In this communion of life, which is the ultimate form of hospitality, there is no logical demarcation between host and guest. The power of life integrates different partners into a cosmic harmony that can produce meaning in the face of the disintegrating power of the increasingly entropic condition of the universe. As human beings we can acknowledge the experience of this harmony in us and in relation to the source of that life in God without, however, negating its manifestation in any other particular organism.

On the other hand, a positive affirmation of the cosmic presence of this healing and harmonizing power of life is expressed in our prayers of praise and thanksgiving. Ancient Christian tradition, through the thanksgiving prayer before and after the meal, considered the eating of food a sacramental act, a continuation of the eucharistic meal. The hospitable sharing of the ordinary meal with the poor and the needy as well as with friends and strangers provides the proper context for the eucharistic meal. The meal is not consumed in gluttonous greed and arrogant selfishness, but in transparent and shared joyfulness and the humility of the total person before the gift of God.

The spiritual crisis underlying consumerism is that material goods are no longer recognized as gifts which require thanksgiving, but as industrial products created by efficient human technology and acquired through the power of money in successful economic systems. In the case of natural food cultivated, harvested and prepared by direct human labour in traditional societies, this recognition is probably easier; there is a sense of hospitality in which the human beings are graciously received and are filled with the good things of the earth. Whether you recognize a personal God or not, communion with nature in the sacred act of eating and drinking certainly belongs to a transcendental order of experience in these societies.

What the pilgrim executes by the act of displacing himself or herself is not rejecting the world as evil or irrelevant, but rediscovering its fundamental transparency to the source of life. Unveiling nature beneath the many sheaths of parochial shelter and aggressive culture, conceptual frames and intellectual constructions, the pilgrim stands with naked feet, in flesh-to-flesh contact with nature, which becomes not just an aggregate of locations but a vast bush that burns and radiates the presence of God.

NOTES

[1] Clement of Rome, *The First Epistle to the Corinthians,* 1.
[2] *The Epistle of Mathetes to Diognetes,* VI.
[3] Antoine Guillaumont, *Aux origines du monachisme chrétien,* Spiritualité orientale, no 30, Paris, 1979, provides an excellent analysis of this theme from the perspective of religious phenomenology.
[4] *Ibid.,* p.108.
[5] Benedicta Ward, tr., *The Sayings of the Desert Fathers,* p.17.
[6] *Ibid.,* p.196.
[7] Thomas W. Ogletree, *Hospitality to the Stranger,* Philadelphia, Fortress, 1985, p.1.
[8] *Ibid.,* p.2.
[9] *Ibid.,* p.58.

4. Silence, Tears and Madness

Christian spirituality has its origin and justification in God's self-emptying act in Christ. Christian experience and practice arising from the compassionate and self-sacrificing love of God constitute the core of what we sometimes vaguely call Christian spirituality. Although the primary emphasis of this spirituality is not on words and concepts, they can be integrated into a sane and holistic experience of reality. Though in the depth of experience words fall short, they still serve a limited function.

Profound reluctance to speak about God and the need for deep, tangible spiritual experience are mutually sustaining. Christian spirituality in the ascetic-monastic tradition essentially sought the spiritual energy produced by the interaction of these two elements. Since this search became paradigmatic for the spiritual tradition of the church, especially in the East, we may mention a few constitutive elements of it which are not well known. Silence, tears and madness belong to what we may call the archaeology of the Spirit. A sympathetic perception of their significance in building up the Christian tradition can facilitate the "dialogue of cultures" within the ecumenical movement.

Hesychia — the silence of being

The Sayings of the Desert Fathers, a highly influential work in Eastern Christian spirituality, relates this story from the life of Anthony, the third-century Egyptian pioneer of the ascetic movement:

> Three Fathers used to go and visit blessed Anthony every year, and two of them used to discuss their thoughts and the salvation of their souls with him, but the third always remained silent and did not ask him anything. After a long time, Abba Anthony said to him, "You often come here to see me, but you never ask me anything," and the other replied, "It is enough for me to see you, Father."[1]

Silence, which we have seen earlier as the apophatic negation of words and concepts about the mystery of God, has been made the cornerstone of the great Christian spiritual tradition that originated in the Egyptian and Syro-Palestinian deserts and flowed out of the confines of deserts to shape the spiritual, liturgical and theological ethos of the churches in many places.

The profound inner silence of being or *hesychia* (stillness) is not just emptiness or absence of mental and emotional activity.

Out of the depth of silence emerges the figure of the self-emptying saint. This spiritually luminous person creates a presence and radiates an energy by his or her very being. The silent monk in the story of Anthony is spiritually nourished and enlightened by the very presence of the person of the great ascetic. For him it is a vision that requires no conversation or reasoning.

To our contemporary minds this accent on silence and presence might appear too passive and devoid of any impulse towards Christian social and ethical praxis. However, without attempting to reduce all Christian spiritual experience to an external activist mode, one may still discover some deep connections between this spiritual tradition, which developed within the body of the church and became an integral element of the total Christian experience, and some genuine concerns of the contemporary world.

The ascetic-monastic movement transformed the negation of speech in theology into a positive spirituality around *hesychia* or inner stillness. Our immediate interest, however, is not with the techniques of spiritual practice developed in the "hesychast movement" in monastic settlements like Mount Athos, but in the spiritual potential of silence to accomplish the transition from negation to affirmation.[2] The affirmation, however, is not principally in definitions and concepts, but in a life of constant creative prayer and deep compassion for all. As Kallistos Ware affirms on the authority of the patristic tradition:

> The way of *hesychia* lies open to all: the one thing needful is inner silence, not outer. And though this inner silence presupposes the "laying aside" of images in prayer, the final effect of this negation is to assert with fresh vividness the ultimate value of all things and all persons in God.[3]

In an enlightening article on silence and prayer, Ware interprets the broad significance of *hesychia* in the monastic tradition, moving from the external to the internal sense, relating it to solitude, the spirituality of the monastic call, the more inward notion of return into oneself, spiritual poverty and the Jesus prayer.[4] He also distinguishes the hesychast tradition from seventeenth-century Western quietism, which stressed passivity and the annihilation of will and condemned all human effort. Inner silence in its true form is identified with the unceasing prayer of the Holy Spirit from within (Rom. 8:26) and it denotes the transition from "my prayers" to the "prayer of God" working in me. Ware quotes the beautiful expression of this experience by Isaac the Syrian:

> When the Spirit makes its dwelling place in a man, he does not cease to pray, because the Spirit will constantly pray in him. Then, neither when he sleeps nor when he is awake, will prayer be cut off from his soul; but when he eats and when he drinks, when he lies down or when he does any work, even when he is immersed in sleep, the perfumes of prayer will breathe in his heart spontaneously. [5]

Although the contemplatives and ascetics do not engage in direct activity in the world, their invisible presence and the value of their prayers have been fully acknowledged by the Christian tradition. Their insights and sensitivity to human needs may often far exceed the perception of some of those who are immersed in external activity for the gospel. As Ware puts it: "Men such as St Anthony of Egypt or St Seraphim of Sarov lived for whole decades in all but total silence and physical isolation. Yet the ultimate effect of this isolation was to confer on them clarity of vision and an exceptional compassion." [6]

Silence of being shows itself as true compassion. The whole ascetic-monastic movement, in spite of many shortcomings, was oriented to the acquisition of compassion — the tender mercy and love of God that made incarnation possible.

There is here an eclipse of "theology" in the usual modern sense of discourse on God. Yet the silence of being that is subtly and soothingly audible here shows the way to the incarnate love of God. This silence does not reject the intellectual and the rational or the task of the church to teach, preach, interpret and instruct. Nor does it underestimate the Christian call for justice and human dignity and the church's combat against the forces of evil which take various social and political forms in human society. The silence of being, marked by constant prayer, continual repentance and abiding compassion for all creation, assumes the hidden role of roots that invisibly support and sustain the superstructure of Christian life.

It was perhaps the peculiar genius of the Christian tradition in the past that it could combine, though not without imperfections, the deep concern for justice and human dignity expressed by people like John Chrysostom, Basil of Caesarea and Ambrose of Milan with the self-emptying and compassionate silence of ascetics like Anthony and Isaac the Syrian. Both dimensions were understood to participate in the same mystery of incarnation. If there is any feeling of polarization in our times between the ascetic and the active, between the roots and the trunk, it is a false dichotomy, and the balance must be restored on the model of the union of spirit and matter in the incarnation. There were times — for example, in the wake of the Council of Chalcedon — when the bloody conflicts that arose over *how* the divine and the human were united in the one person of Jesus Christ left very little space for exploring the social and ethical consequences for the life of the world of that "perfect union" (on which both sides agreed) of humanity and divinity. The spiritual aridity created by the proliferation of technical theology was largely compensated by the many silent beings who were continually holding up the world in the presence of God in compassionate prayer.

Although compassion is not exclusively Christian, the Christian understanding of it may be distinguished from that of other religious traditions. In a discussion with Masao Abe of the ethical and historical dimensions of faith, John B. Cobb acknowledges the need for himself as a Christian to relativize the ethical, yet he thinks that the very process deepens the sense of concrete particularity and historical responsibility.[7] In response Abe makes clear that the Buddhist notion of *sunyata* (nothingness) has two aspects: wisdom and compassion. "Wisdom without compassion is not true wisdom. Compassion without wisdom is not true compassion. In contrast to the Buddhist pair of 'wisdom and compassion' the Christian pair is 'love and justice'."[8] While Abe admits that in Christianity love and justice cannot be understood separately one from the other, he equates the Christian notion of love to the Buddhist notion of compassion and says that there is no Buddhist equivalent to the Christian notion of justice and that "overall, Buddhist history shows indifference to social evil".[9]

This statement may apply more or less to other Asian religions like Hinduism, even though it has a very profound notion of *dharma* which includes justice, responsibility and right order at the personal and cosmic levels. Compared to the prophetic tradition in Semitic religions, Asian religions do not seem to manifest any sharp sensitivity to social evil. Whether this difference in attitude has something to do with the notion of deity as personal or impersonal could be an interesting area of research.

Indian historian Romila Thapar has remarked that "the fundamental sanity of Indian civilization has been due to an absence of Satan"[10] — in other words, of a personified principle of evil. Naturally, this absence is the counterpart to the absence of a personal God. Perhaps one could argue that those religions which have a notion of deity as personal and a principle of evil opposed to it can generate more social dynamism, though it can spill over to aggression and conquest in the name of God. However, there is no conclusive historical evidence that religions like Christianity have consistently shown social concern and sensitivity to social evil. On the contrary, institutional Christianity has often impeded the fruition of many truly Christian values in human society by misusing its power and spiritual authority.

It would be futile to seek to establish the superiority of any religion in this respect. As Christians what is appropriate for us is to base our compassionate commitment to the historical realm and our sense of transcendence on the mystery of God's incarnation in Christ. An infinite space opens up as we meditate on this mystery of union and work out the consequences for our world. Without falling into reductionist paradigms of reality or being confined to systems, we may perceive this foundational event as the key to a holistic understanding of Christian tradition. The silence of countless anonymous, self-effacing human beings, the vigorous spiritual struggles of the ascetic tradition, the eschatological radicalism experimented in monastic communities, the active ethical and social involvement of prophetic Christians in the world, the intellectual struggles of those engaged in theological reflection — all are integral to this holistic vision of the Body of Christ. While these elements may correct and complement each other, they need also to affirm the multiplicity of the ways of the Spirit.

The gift of tears

Prayer is not a disembodied exercise of the mind or intellect. At the deeper levels of prayer, the body and its senses are involved, and prayer becomes an experience of the total person. "Becoming prayer" is a favourite patristic expression. Tears, as an expression of the "sensible" experience, have been always associated with deep compassionate prayer. When the ascetic tradition speaks about "the gift of tears" (*charisma ton dakuron*), it is not as an expression of sentiments, but as a special charism of the Holy Spirit that induces an incessant flow of tears that "make the flesh bloom" (Isaac the Syrian) in joy and compassion.

In a civilization dominated by the objectivity of cold reason, tears are a matter of shame, vulnerability and the expression of subjective and irrational sentiments. So they are censored from public display and banished from all serious intellectual discourse. Christian theology has followed other scientific disciplines in ignoring the value of tears as signs of *metanoia* and signals of a compassionate transcendence. Although tears retain a central place in Eastern Christian spirituality, very few people speak about this openly, as they belong to the hidden side of the spiritual life.

Tears originate at different levels. There are tears of sorrow and grief occurring to every human being sometime or other. This is the primary level of tears springing from our fundamental experience. The new-born child cries (though without tears) at the breaking of the umbilical cord, as it comes out from the cosy womb of the mother. The tear glands begin to secrete later on, about the third month. The cry of the baby signals its need of food or warmth or simply the presence of the mother. Tears here invoke the profound and invisible links the human baby has with other persons and with its surroundings.

In spiritual practice one speaks of the tears of contrition or repentance.[11] This is the phenomenon of tears transformed to the spiritual plane. Sin alienates us and breaks the umbilical cord from God and fellow human beings, and the repenting person weeps in sorrow over this separation.

There is another level of tears in the spiritual tradition of the Christian East: tears of compassion. God's tender mercy and love enter the whole being of a person and that person melts into tears which continually flow in compassionate love for God's creation.

"The gift of tears" is not necessarily reserved for a spiritual elite but, as Gregory of Nazianzus affirms, is open to all, though everyone has his or her special gifts.[12] For Gregory tears are a fifth baptism, "a more laborious one" than the baptism of Moses in the Red Sea, of John in the Jordan, of Jesus in the Spirit or of martyrs by blood.

For Symeon the New Theologian (949-1022), tears carry a powerful baptismal significance for spiritual regeneration, which purifies and illumines the inner person. In tears "one drinks the grace of the Holy Spirit who unites us in Christ".[13] As a second baptism it washes away the dirt that accumulates in us after baptism.

Tears can be a sign of deep repentance, but great discernment is needed to judge the level of the inner state of the spiritual seeker. Tears can appear in a beginner as well as one who is advanced in spiritual life. Deep penitence (*penthos*) is not simply an act of will, but is intimately connected to bodily sensibility. J. Hausherr points out that penitence as an act of will is not necessarily a physical experience, while *penthos* in the Eastern tradition is always linked to the shedding of tears, a profound bodily sensation.[14] Isaac the Syrian places tears at the border line between our physical and spiritual natures. Tears mediate between the material and the spiritual and signify the stage of transition from one to the other.

Although tears in a spiritual person begin with compunction, repentance for one's sins, sadness over the alienation from God, terror of coming judgment and fear of God, they rise to the higher levels of compassion and genuine love. John Climacus contrasts tears of love with tears of fear. In Isaac the Syrian, compassion and tears of love open up to embrace the whole of created reality, including those elements which are usually thought to be inimical to human life. In a celebrated passage, the bishop of Nineveh is asked: "What is a compassionate heart?" He answers:

> The heart that is inflamed in this way embraces the entire creation — man, birds, animals and even demons. At the recollection of them, and at the sight of them, such a man's eyes fill with tears that arise from the great compassion which presses on his heart. The heart grows tender and cannot endure to hear of or look upon any injury or even the smallest suffering inflicted upon anything in creation. For this reason such a man prays increasingly with tears even for irrational animals and for the enemies of truth

and for all who harm it, that they may be guarded and be forgiven. The compassion which pours out from his heart without measure, like God's, extends even to reptiles.[15]

Praying in compassion for even the demons is certainly radical Christianity. Yet it is simply the imitation of the forgiving love on the cross that penetrates every atom of created reality. It affirms the essential goodness and integrity of all that has come into existence through God's will. In this depth of compassionate love, one cannot but pray even for the demonic forces that disrupt the integrity of God's creation. Even they can be transfigured and integrated to what is true and good by the mellowing and illuminating oil of compassion.

One may remember here that in the Eastern patristic view, evil is not a substantially positive force, but the absence of the good, as darkness is the absence of light. "Evil has no substance or kingdom," said Gregory of Nazianzus. Deep compassionate prayer can radiate the power of light that illumines all parts of creation and eliminates the non-being of evil.

The best authorities in the spiritual tradition would maintain that a true ascetic aspires to nothing but the experience of the love of God. This experience invariably translates itself into a compassionate heart — a heart that bleeds at the pain of any being anywhere in the world and prays in tears, a heart that rejoices at every glow of joy in creation and renders thanks to God in profound gratitude. It is not doctrinal orthodoxy as an intellectual notion that primarily characterizes the saint, but the spirit of love and praise, manifested in a heart full of compassion. So a true saint may be received beyond the conceptual walls of doctrine. A good example in the Eastern tradition is Isaac the Syrian. Though consecrated bishop of Nineveh in the East Syrian Church associated with the name of Nestorius, who was condemned as a heretic at the Ecumenical Council of Ephesus in 431, Isaac is venerated as one of the eminent spiritual teachers in the Orthodox tradition.

Tears of compassion constitute a prism which reveals the other to us in a completely new light. As tears have the purgative powers of wiping off the stains of prejudice, hostility and cold indifference that distort our normal vision, they reveal the resplendent seal of God's image in every being.

Christian theology speaks volumes about the foundational gift of the image of God to the human person, individually and collectively, but often shies away from harvesting the implications of this for concrete life in community, between nations, between people of different faiths and cultural contexts, between the rich and the poor. We are unable to spell out in theological categories what it is that links the human person as the image of God to the rest of creation. We can only affirm, in a strictly anthropocentric way, partly negatively, that human beings are created in the image of God while animals and plants are not. Yet it is also integral to our faith to affirm that *all things visible and invisible* come from the same source, the creator of all. If all things are born of the same matrix of God, out of the same divine will and love, all carry the stamp of God's being. Theological speculation, however sophisticated, finds it difficult to articulate positively the connecting link without falling into some kind of pantheistic holism. It can only negatively indicate the distinction. A compassionate heart, however, discerns the deep ligaments of divine love that unite humanity with the rest of creation. As St Silvan the Athonite puts it: "The heart that has learned to love has compassion for all creation." This is not to obliterate the difference between humanity and the rest of creation, but to affirm that human beings are created to be a sacrament of love for the whole creation and witnesses to the love of God that continually sustains the created world.

Eastern Christian spirituality is nourished by the stories of saintly men and women and their experience of God and compassion for the world. An age that narrowly concentrates on ethical and social activism tends to underestimate the invisible roots of cosmic compassion gleaming through such traditional and apparently pious hagiographies. It is, however, a welcome sign that in the new search for spiritual and cultural roots in various contextual theologies, story-telling as revelatory human experience is again assuming a prominent role.

Stories of saintly persons living in peaceful harmony with nature, even with wild animals, are not mere fiction, but indicate the deepest human aspiration for holistic existence, rooted in the real experience of individual human beings. Isaac the Syrian speaks about this wonderful harmony with nature experienced by the "humble man", the human being who lives in the kenotic humility of God devoid of all trappings of an inflated ego, reminiscent of the pre-fallen Adam:

> He who speaks contemptuously against the humble man, and does not consider him an animate creature, is like one who has opened his mouth against God. And though the humble man is contemptible in his eyes, his honour is esteemed by all creation. The humble man approaches ravening beasts, and when their gaze rests upon him, their wildness is tamed. They come up to him as to their Master, wag their heads and tails and lick his hands and feet, for they smell coming from him that same scent that exhaled from Adam before the fall, when they were gathered together before him and he gave them names in Paradise. This was taken away from us, but Jesus has renewed it, and given it back to us through his coming. This it is which has sweetened the fragrance of the race of men. [16]

Humanity can taste this harmony only when it learns to discern, far beyond its self-interest in survival, the roots of all life in God's self-emptying love.

What Dostoevsky says through the words of Father Zosima in *The Brothers Karamazov* reflects the genuine conviction and experience of many in the best of Christian spiritual tradition:

> Love all God's creation, the whole of it and every grain of sand. Love every leaf, every ray of God's light! Love the animals, love the plants, love everything. If you love everything, you will perceive the divine mystery in things. And once you have perceived it, you will begin to comprehend it ceaselessly, more and more every day. And you will at last come to love the whole world with an abiding universal love. Love the animals: God has given them the rudiments of thought and untroubled joy. Do not, therefore, trouble them, do not torture them, do not deprive them of their joy, do not go against God's intent.

Tears of compassion have helped many to experience the life-creating and life-fostering parenthood of God beyond the gender-based discriminations of biological fatherhood and motherhood. Since the deepest urge of love is to create and preserve life, those who enter the zone of life in compassion will always seek to foster life wherever it is found and in whatever form it appears. While biological parenthood, especially motherhood, in every species seeks to preserve its own species in a possessively and aggressively protective way over against other species and at times against some members of its own species, the way of tears points one to the source where no flicker of life is quenched.

Humanity can be a privileged sacrament and witness of God's love. Only recently have many Christian theologians begun to perceive that the survival and salvation of the human species alone is a totally inadequate basis for any sensible theological ethical discourse. Although some streams of Christian tradition have sustained an alternate hermeneutic of the Scriptures and perceived truth in the tears of love for all life, they have often been slighted by the imperious missionary search for a unique theology to present the unique Christ to the unbelieving pagan world. The greater the drive "to redeem the world", the narrower the basis of Christian theology and social praxis. Many Christians now take upon themselves in good faith the ecological responsibility of "redeeming God's creation", which would in all probability prove counterproductive and catastrophic to creation, simply because the fundamental framework of our theological triumphalism, marked by cultural hubris and the drive to dominate, and our solely human-centred survival motives remain unchallenged. In such a frame of mind, expressions like "the gift of tears" or "self-emptying love" may not convey any meaning. Tears might simply indicate weakness, vulnerability and incompetence. They may at best be understood as metaphors from a distant past. Conquest and compassion are at opposite poles, and the worlds of meaning they carry stand far apart. The "gift of tears" signals the alternate way of the Spirit.

Fools for Christ's sake

The unusual ascetic-prophetic phenomenon of so-called "holy fools" in the history of the church exemplifies a radical attempt to live a self-emptying life on the model of divine kenosis in the humiliated Christ. This was a peculiar form of spirituality lived by some ascetics, who appeared insane to outsiders but voluntarily took upon themselves the cross of Christ and deprived themselves of the comforts of a normal life.

Folly for Christ's sake is known in both East and West, but it is in the Eastern tradition that it is recognized as a special charisma of the Spirit and an extraordinary form of sanctity, particularly in Russian Orthodox spirituality.

The well-known figure of the "holy fool" (*jurodivyj*) in the spiritual history of Russia exemplifies the close intertwining of the images of pilgrim and prophet, mystic and vagabond, ascetic and alien. Russian literary and spiritual history is profoundly marked by the wandering "fools for the sake of Christ" who criss-crossed the length and breadth of the Russian soil. The tradition flourished in sixteenth-century Russia and became an inalienable part of the Orthodox spiritual tradition. The kenosis of Christ, his voluntary self-abnegation for the sake of humanity, is the basis and model for this spirituality of self-humiliation. As Michel Evdokimov puts it, the very first fool for the sake of God was God himself, who out of love and compassion for humanity assumed the humblest of human conditions in the incarnate Christ. [17]

The fool for Christ's sake (the Russian word means a miserable wretch, the Greek equivalent *salos* implies an agitator or troublemaker) has biblical basis in the self-understanding of St Paul, as one who has become a fool to the world in order to follow Christ. He understood this folly as the mark of the apostles of Christ:

> For I think that God has exhibited us apostles as last of all, as though sentenced to death, because we have become a spectacle to the world, to angels and to mortals. We are fools for the sake of Christ, but you are wise in Christ. We are weak, but you are strong. You are held in honour, but we in disrepute. To the present hour we are hungry and thirsty, we are poorly clothed and beaten and homeless, and we grow weary from the work of our own hands. When reviled, we bless; when persecuted, we endure; when slandered, we speak kindly. We have become like the rubbish of the world, the dregs of all things to this very day (1 Cor. 4:9-13).

This is what the well-known fools like St Simeon in the sixth century and St Basil the Blessed in the sixteenth, and women fools like Xenia of St Petersburg in the eighteenth century and Pasha of Sarov in our own century tried to imitate out of love for Christ and for the people. They rejected the wisdom and security of this world and became fools in search of true wisdom. Their self-assumed madness was a heroic endeavour not to conform to the shape and standards of the present age which is passing (1 Cor. 3:18).

The call of the kingdom of God was the driving force for the apparently abnormal way of life they followed. As John Saward puts it: "The most important element in folly for Christ's sake is the eschatological, the conflict between the sensibility, values and structures of this present world and those of the world to come."[18] The vision of the coming age, however, did not discourage them from involvement in society, particularly defending the poor and the marginalized. The prophetic zeal of the holy fools was the direct outcome of their awareness of the contrast between the two realities. As Christos Yannaras makes clear, "The fool is the charismatic man who has direct experience of the new reality of the kingdom of God and undertakes to demonstrate in a prophetic way the antithesis of this present world with the world of the kingdom."[19]

Prophetic zeal and fearlessness in face of injustice, combined with tears and tender compassion for the poor victims of political and economic oppression and social marginalization, characterized the holy fools. These particular traits arose directly out of their practice of total non-possession, the literal condition of being an exile and a true pilgrim. They slept in the streets and the porches of churches like the most destitute of beggars. They wore rags in comical ways and sometimes went naked in order to provide shock therapy to the moral hypocrites of society. They consciously assumed the condition of insanity and challenged the bastions of authority whenever it became oppressive to the poor. Their state of assumed madness and ascetic detachment made them elusive to the custodians of law and order. It is said that Basil the Blessed used to throw stones angrily at the houses of the decadent rich and with great compassion kiss the doors of the houses of prostitutes.

The fool for Christ's sake totally identified with the miserable and the outcasts to the extent of shocking the moral and spiritual sense of "normal" Christians. St Simeon offended "good" Christians and exposed their hypocrisy by publicly eating meat on Good Friday or dancing with the prostitutes, staying overnight in their houses and sharing the life of the most wretched on the earth. Simeon was a strict ascetic who comes to the community to bear witness in a preposterous way to the love of Christ. As Saward puts it:

> Simeon has learned the terrible goodness of the Lord in silence and solitude and now comes to share it with the wretched of the earth in the streets, taverns and brothels of the city. And the strength which supports Simeon in his wild life of folly, in his dances with harlots and his fellowship with the depraved, is the *apatheia* of the wilderness, which is not a crude insensitivity to physical stimulation, but an emancipation of the senses whereby man ceases to be an automaton, a victim of compulsive behaviour, and becomes sovereignly free in his relations with others, refusing to see them as objects of possession and exploitation. [20]

In the example of St Basil the Blessed, the self-emptying love of God as the driving force of prophetic concern for liberating justice and the dispossessing identification with the poor of the world again stands in sharp relief. Western travellers to Russia like Gilles Fletcher (1588) bore witness to the powerful way in which Basil, who walked naked in the streets of Moscow, challenged the authority of the state. Nicolas, another holy fool, is said to have publicly offered to Ivan the Terrible a piece of raw meat dripping with blood to remind him of his bloody massacre at Novgorod and the many acts of injustice he committed against people. [21]

The fools for Christ's sake voluntarily accepted humiliation and deprivation, remembering that Christ had been insulted and beaten up. They showed in their lives the vulnerability of God who accepted suffering and death in Christ for the sake of humanity. They wandered homeless in search of their true home. The essence of this holy folly, according to Kologrivof, consisted "in taking voluntarily on oneself humiliations and insults, in order to increase humility, meekness and kindness of heart, and so to develop love, even for one's enemies and persecutors". [22]

Arising basically from the ascetic-monastic movement, the folly voluntarily assumed by many men and women is still a source of inspiration to spiritual seekers. By officially recognizing the authenticity of this form of spirituality, the church placed itself in the critical light of the kingdom of God. The preposterous character of the gospel which removes the yoke of oppression from people, which heals the sick and shows compassion to all alike, is affirmed by the tradition of the church. By this bold act of accepting folly for Christ's sake, the church declares that it has no reason not to be engaged in the people's struggles to restore justice and dignity to all human beings created in the image of God. The tenderness of heart at which the whole ascetic-monastic tradition aimed, exemplifying the aspiration of the whole people of God, renders this involvement not an isolated political-ideological combat, but an overwhelming striving "for the kingdom of God and his righteousness" (Matt. 6:33). This was gospel radicalism at its deepest.

NOTES

1 Benedicta Ward, tr., *The Sayings of the Desert Fathers,* p.6.

2 Elizabeth Behr-Sigel, *The Place of the Heart*, Torrance, California, Oakwood Publications, 1992.

3 Kallistos Ware, "Silence in Prayer: The Meaning of Hesychia", in A.M. Allchin, ed., *Theology and Prayer*, London, Fellowship of St Alban and St Sergius, 1975, pp.8-28.

4 *Ibid.*

5 *Mystic Treatises*, quoted by Ware, *ibid.*, p.16.

6 *Ibid.*

7 J. Cobb and C. Ives, *The Emptying God*, p.179.

8 *Ibid.*

9 *Ibid.*

10 R. Thapar, *A History of India*, Harmondsworth, Penguin, 1987, Vol. I, p.15; cf. K.M. George, "Nation as Monastery: Need for a New Political Askesis", in K.M. Tharakan, ed., *Triune God: Love, Justice and Peace*, Mavelikkara, India, 1989, p.156.

11 See M. Lot-Borodine, "Le mystère du 'don des larmes' dans l'Orient chrétien", in O. Clément et al., *La douloureuse joie*, Abbaye de Bellefontaine, 1981.

12 Gregory of Nazianzus, *Oration* 39:17.

13 Symeon the New Theologian, quoted by Lot-Borodine, *loc. cit.*, p.175.

14 I. Hausherr, *Penthos: La doctrine de la componction dans l'orient chrétien*, Rome, 1944, p.31-32.

15 Isaac of Nineveh, quoted in Seely Beggiani, *Introduction to Eastern Christian Spirituality: The Syriac Tradition*, Montrose, USA, Ridge Row Press, 1991, p.75.

16 Isaac the Syrian, *Homily* 77.

17 Michel Evdokimov, *Pèlerins russes*, Paris, Cerf, 1987, p.50

18 John Saward, "The Fool for Christ's Sake in Monasticism, East and West", in Allchin, *op. cit.*, pp.29-55; see also his *Perfect Fools: Folly for Christ's Sake in Catholic and Orthodox Spirituality*, Oxford University Press, 1980.

19 Quoted by Saward in Allchin, *op. cit.*, p.31.

20 *Ibid.*, p.34.

21 Irina Goraïnoff, *Les fols en Christ*, Paris, Desclée de Brouwer, 1983, p.91.

22 Quoted by Saward, *loc. cit.*, p.33.

5. The Silent Roots

Rediscovering the total life of the church and celebrating it together is a fundamental ecumenical task for our times. In their separate development East and West have produced great traditions of theological reflection and spiritual practices. They also retain a memory of the undivided common tradition. While no one today would seriously question the legitimacy of developing particular theological and spiritual ways of understanding the Christian faith in particular social and cultural contexts, it is a cause of concern when our different perceptions divide the one body of Christ and its unity of faith in the one Christ. The modern ecumenical movement came into being precisely because the division in the church, the one body of Christ, was shown to be a counter-witness to the proclamation of the life-giving gospel. Protestant, Orthodox and Roman Catholic families of churches unequivocally affirm the need for unity, though there are still wide differences among these traditions about the nature of that unity.

One inevitable limitation of the ecumenical movement as it appears today is its almost exclusive focus on the tangible, visible part of tradition represented in institutional forms, doctrines, creeds, confessions and structures of administration. Important as these are, they represent the historical reality of our churches, partly in their unity and partly in their division. The quest for visible unity must of course address itself to this explicit tradition of the church. However, the infra-tradition of the life of the church is hidden from ordinary ecumenical view. This is not a passive infrastructure. Real spiritual combat can take place in this realm. Every aspiration to unity must refer primarily to this root tradition of Christian life and experience, because this is where constant struggle, pain, suffering and tears for the sake of the unity of the church and for the harmony of humanity and of all creation happen. Our usual "confessional" attitude to each other's doctrinal positions cannot always penetrate to this realm or appreciate its regenerative and renewing powers. Nor can we place it as a programme or project on the ecumenical agenda.

So a plea for consideration of the significance of the total life of the church for the ecumenical movement is a plea for a deeper and more holistic awareness of the total experience of the people of God, of members of the Body of Christ individually and corporately in all ages and in all places. A silent sigh of deep prayer, a glass of cold water to a needy one, an empathetic tear drop of compassionate solidarity, a fast or vigil for the sake of love, a poetic meditation on the word of God, a smile of encouragement, the painting of an icon of divine hospitality — any of these may seem banal and insignificant beside epoch-making councils or heroic acts of martyrdom or world gatherings of Christian churches. Yet they too are constitutive of what we call the Christian tradition.

But how do we reckon with the millions of such little acts of faith and love in silence and self-abnegation in the present moment? By deep awareness, we do not mean that one should keep all these things at the level of consciousness. Rather we mean the undergirding sense of being rooted in and nourished by this complex life-experience of the Christian community, existing in space and time yet fully open to the mystery of being beyond.

The Eastern Christian tradition keeps this in the image of the mother church — the all-remembering mother, who like the Virgin Mary, "treasures up all these things in her heart" (Luke 2:51). Mary becomes the symbol par excellence of the mother church, of humanity and of the whole of creation. Just as Mary, who becomes Theotokos, mother of God, by the constitutive action of the Holy Spirit, bears Christ and yet is saved by Christ, the church's very being is constituted by the Holy Spirit. The church is enabled to bear Christ for the world and is saved through the cross and resurrection of Christ. The christological and the pneumatological become normative and constitutive for understanding the church as the bearer of the total tradition. The eucharistic *anamnesis*, the great "remembrance" of the church, takes care of all that is apparently the least and the last.

Ecclesiology is a permanent source of misunderstanding between East and West in ecumenical discussions, particularly between the Orthodox and the Protestants. The institutional and historical dimensions of "the congregation of the faithful" are never the primary components of the church in the mind of the Orthodox East. The East tends to personify the church as the mother who conceives and brings up her children in the inner, intuitive, almost uterine knowledge of the mystery of the triune God and of the incarnation of Christ. The historical, chronological development of the Christian community is subsumed by the image of an all-embracing, all-remembering and all-suffering mother in the liturgical and spiritual vision of the East. The church is also organically understood, following the Pauline image, as the Body of Christ which shares in everything that the incarnate Christ experienced from his baptism to his death and resurrection. The vision in the Book of Revelation of the heavenly Jerusalem descending like a bride adorned for her husband is again the self-understanding of the church, reminding her of her trans-historical calling. The image of a new creation by the Holy Spirit at Pentecost, a community of the Spirit that is not regulated or governed by purely sociological norms and historical structures, is also central to the Eastern church's self-understanding. The list of such components that go into the making of the Eastern ecclesiology can be very long, if one goes through all the biblical and liturgical texts. Yet they do not exhaust the mystery of the church, because the church as the Body of Christ is rooted in the mystery of the triune God.

This seems to constitute the perennial misunderstanding between the East and the West on the question of the church. The Western Protestant tradition has a clear, historical, down-to-earth approach to the "phenomenon" of the Christian church, which is seldom personified by the use of metaphors to any personal or aesthetic levels (though the New Testament authors did so) but simply referred to as the impersonal, objective, institutional "it" out there to be criticized, renewed and reshaped, taking seriously current sociological and anthropological trends. This view of the church takes its origin from the act of God in history, and continually refers to history and remains acutely aware of the "con-temporary" world in the literal sense of that term. The ethical and social involvement of the church flows out of this immediate consciousness of the present, almost to the virtual exclusion of the past and the unplanned future. To Orthodox Christians this appears to be a certain sense of justification by the works done in history.

Perhaps we have pushed both views to the extreme, yet they carry some truth. The extremes simply can show us the major thrust of these traditions, though the ecclesial self-understanding of the Orthodox East and the Protestant West are far more complex, and are capable of great internal diversity. The ecumenical movement has exposed them to each other, though real mutual understanding still remains elusive.

One example of how these two traditions travel along parallel tracks is the question frequently asked: Can the church repent? In ecumenical statements, the Protestant tradition finds it quite natural and theological to say categorically that "the church must repent". On the Orthodox side there is an instinctive resistance to that statement. How can the one, holy, catholic and apostolic mother church, the body of Christ, repent?

Some Orthodox would bluntly say that the Protestant statement reflects a purely sociological understanding of the church without any sense of its deeper reality. In response some Protestants would say that the Orthodox have no sense of the historical-ethical dimension and that they have a very abstract, idealistic and unworkable notion of the church. The misunderstanding originates in the fundamental imagery or lack of it sustained by their respective traditions. Where is the truth?

The Orthodox tradition is, in fact, soaked in the idea of repentance. It affirms that a Christian must constantly repent. All the fasts, vigils, prayers and other ascetic disciplines are special occasions for intense repentance. The prayers in the Great Lent constantly remind the people to repent and be converted. In the monastic tradition, the monks understood their whole life as dedicated to prayer and repentance. The difference in the Eastern tradition, however, is that, according to the liturgical texts, it is always the mother church who calls her children to repentance, to turn to the Father, the source of all life. The mother is intensely interceding on behalf of all her children. Inspired by the Spirit, the church participates in the high priestly prayer of Christ, by offering the whole creation through Christ to the Father and rendering thanks for all the gifts of God. This intercession of the people of God as one body, the Body of Christ, and the call for repentance made by the church to her children cannot be reduced to easily analyzable rational propositions. It is to be perceived rather as a never-ceasing movement of the whole creation oriented to the source of light, illumined and transfigured by the ineffable glory of the triune God.

The challenge for the Orthodox, however, is to manifest the power of this unceasing *metanoia* (repentance, conversion) and the great movement to *theosis* (divinization) built into the very being of the church in addressing the social evils and demonic power structures of our time. To put it in another way, the challenge is to inspire and lead humanity in the path of the kingdom and its justice. The Orthodox tradition has no dearth of resources, spiritual and theological, to work out the implications of the justice of the kingdom in repentance and in the spirit of God's compassion and love.

The beautiful Pauline metaphor of Christ, the bridegroom consecrating and cleansing the church by water and word, so as to present the church to himself in splendour, "without a spot or wrinkle or anything of the kind... holy and without blemish" (Eph. 5:26-27), implies the continuous growth of the church to perfection in Christ. This process of growing and perfecting inevitably involves history. It is a history in which good plants and weeds grow intermingled. The church's movement to meet the bridegroom involves the fostering of the good and the elimination of evil in our earthly existence. However, it is not the sole social "project" of the church as an end in itself, nor is the church the sole actor in history. The Holy Spirit who constantly works to guide all to all truth is the actor with the church in a synergic unity. The Orthodox tradition is profoundly aware that renewing the creation is the "project" of the Holy Spirit and not of any human social or ecclesiastical agency. The ancient Syrian liturgy of St James qualifies the Spirit as "the one who perfects everything that is, and that is to be". The church humbly includes herself in this process of perfecting by the Spirit as she continually invokes the Holy Spirit (*epiclesis*) to indwell and sanctify the whole creation.

The encounter with the Protestant tradition in the ecumenical movement has stimulated several Orthodox churches to conceive their social-ethical vision in more concrete terms. Expectation of a reciprocal enrichment is only natural. In view of a deeper ecumenical understanding, the Protestant tradition will have to develop a higher sensitivity to the ecclesiological vision of the Eastern tradition which, the Orthodox genuinely believe, belongs to the authentic, undivided tradition. Some observations in this regard may be in order:

a) The poetic and aesthetic language of Orthodox theology (and of biblical authors) is not a peripheral decoration but says something about reality. Literal statements, however sophisticated and ecumenical, cannot always convey the full flavour of truth. They objectify truth, and it comes out stale and dead and devoid of its essential aroma. Even the Nicene Creed, when taken out of its doxological and eucharistic context, can be a lifeless statement about the life-giving mystery of God. In the ecumenical movement we have perhaps reached a saturation point in statement-making, still leaving vital truths untouched. If it is an art, then we should be willing occasionally to use the devices of art when we make statements about matters on which we essentially agree, like Christian repentance and conversion and our Christian responsibility to God's world and so on. Truth may at best be hinted at and not stated by our language. And for hinting at the truth, the art of poetic and liturgical language is far more suitable than the prosaic and the purely rational.

b) The words "history" and "historical" can also create misunderstanding. The Orthodox sometimes suspect that the West uses history in a functional and reductionist way, on a strictly linear chronological scale. At best, it becomes the arena of human activity into which God makes occasional interventions. Any distant suggestion of reducing the church to such a historical frame evokes mistrust in the Orthodox partner. While it is generally acknowledged that the Western understanding of linear, evolutionist history has proved itself to be efficient in terms of political-economic expansion and scientific-technological progress, there are still peoples on earth who cannot in all honesty appropriate that model of history. The main reason is that this model, despite its claim to be universal, is oppressively exclusivist. Not only does it leave out the ecosystem and other human cultures as of no interest, but it uses its exclusivism to exploit and destroy them, culminating in a threat to the very survival of human and non-human life on earth.

History thus becomes simply the history of a certain people and their understanding and activities in a certain period of the life of the world. Such a reductionist view is often the unexamined assumption behind most of our discourse on commitment to history.

Orthodox theologians point out that the icon of the Pentecost in the Byzantine tradition exemplifies a different sense of history.[1] In the celebrated motif of this icon St Paul is seated along with the other apostles as they receive the Holy Spirit. Obviously, this does not accord with the chronological order of events as reported in Acts of the Apostles. The iconographer, however, shows that the church's holistic understanding of history supersedes the linear, chronological order. Past, present and future are together present in the presence of the kingdom.

The Orthodox would gladly acknowledge that history in its larger sense is "enfolded" in the being of the church because the body of Christ is inclusive of all and stands in the presence of God on behalf of all creation. Here the understanding of the church goes beyond historical confines, so that any attempt to limit the nature and mission of the church to merely ethical projects or legal structures arising from history will be seen as compromising its eschatological character. Here the challenge for the Orthodox tradition is to reaffirm the creative link between the church's kenotic vocation in the world following the model of the incarnate Christ and its eschatological character as the "new Jerusalem" descending from above. This creative link is nothing other than the bond between the humiliating death of Christ in the world for the sake of the world and the glorious resurrection in which Christ lifts up Adam and Eve from the domain of death.

c) The Western spiritual and intellectual tradition has always been fond of the categories "active" and "passive". Even within the Roman Catholic monastic tradition, one finds the distinction between "active" and "contemplative" monks or nuns. In the Eastern tradition — though one can find the distinction between *praxis* and *theoria* in the patristic writings — no aspect of the life of the church was qualified as either active or passive.

Perhaps we need to re-examine the whole notion of passivity and activity in this ecologically sensitive age. Nature has been assumed to be passive in relation to human beings who are active. Culture and civilizational process have thus been understood as the product of human activity on passive nature. With the onset of the environmental crisis we began to perceive that nature had not been passive at all. The nemesis of nature has goaded human beings into an awareness, though minimal, of the truth that human life will be threatened unless we take the non-human world as an active partner in the fostering of life. Human aggressivity towards nature was directly proportional to the depth of our conviction that nature was passive. Feminist thinkers tell us that the same attitude is maintained by human males in patriarchal societies with regard to women. The so-called passivity of women is interpreted as a free space for masculine domination. The idea of equal partnership of two active beings is almost totally ignored in the social and legal structures governing men-women relationships.

Definitions of "active" and "passive" are the products of a culture centred on the pre-eminence of dominant, aggressive egotism. Freedom was largely understood as the freedom of speech and movement. Nature, lacking this freedom, was qualified as passive. In the case of women, the reverse movement applied: they were qualified as passive and denied the freedom of speech and mobility.

In recovering the total tradition, we need to obliterate these convenient yet misleading categories of active and passive. The "infra-tradition", though silent and invisible, is fully participating in the work of God.

d) Ecumenical dialogue between different Christian traditions and between Christianity and other religions now takes place largely at the conceptual-theological level. While this is necessary when two different worldviews, each with its heavy baggage of cultural, religious and philosophical perceptions, agree to seek mutual understanding, such intellectual dialogue cannot take us beyond a certain point. This is because the conceptual framework and theological formulation used to communicate a faith-universe necessarily fall short of the experience of truth that it really holds. That experience is sustained by the silent roots, which refuse access to conceptual and verbal language.

The dilemma is that a true dialogue which can penetrate the walls of intellectual categories and linguistic constructions to reach the roots tends to be silent and to break with definitions that divide. Matthew Fox expresses the quality of roots thus:

> All spirituality is about roots. For all spirituality is about living a nonsuperficial and therefore a deep, rooted, or radical (from *radix*, root) life. Roots are collective and not merely personal — much less are they private or individualized. To get in touch with spiritual roots is truly to leave the private quest for my roots to get

in touch with our roots. Where roots grow and nourish in the bowels of the earth, there things come together and there a collectivity of energies is shared. No root that was ruggedly individualistic would long survive. In the earth's bowels roots feed on the same organisms as they twist and turn interdependently among one another. The name we give this collectivity of roots is tradition.[2]

Roots hold a great mystery. Their ways are not known to us. If we try to expose them to the view of all curious passers-by, it is the end of the tree. So roots have to be hidden beneath the earth. They travel great distances in search of water and nutrients. We cannot control them from outside without endangering the health of the tree. We may prune and define the shape of the branches according to our imagination and cultural tastes. But we cannot cut down or limit the freedom of the roots. They sustain the tree in silence and freedom.

In the Christian tradition, the access to the roots is provided by the economy (*oikonomia*) of incarnation. *Oikonomia* is not just the acts of God in history. It is the self-emptying, life-giving space of freedom granted to us in Christ. There we find the roots of our humanity and of our universe, travelling great distances to cross borders and reach out unseen and unheard to the source of life.

NOTES

[1] John Zizioulas, "Eschatology and History", in T. Wieser, ed., *Whither Ecumenism*, Geneva, WCC, 1986, pp.62-71.
[2] Matthew Fox, ed., *Western Spirituality: Historical Roots, Ecumenical Routes*, Notre Dame IN, Fides/Claretian, 1979, p.1.